Border Country

Dr Dennis Lewis

Copyright

ISBN

978-1-8382659-1-5

Publisher

Dr Dennis Lewis

Printed by

Fosseway Press, Radstock

Dedication

This book is dedicated to my sister Anita who was so much of my life growing up in Marshfield.

Key to Map of Marshfield and Surroundings

1. Frank Bevan's Central Stores
2. Post Office
3. 3 Council Houses (Chippenham Road)
4. Almshouses
5. Church Hall
6. Raven's Grocery Shop
7. Doctor's Surgery at Bank House
8. Royal British Legion Club
9. The Crown
10. The Wheel
11. The Lord Nelson
12. Butcher's Shop
13. The Barn
14. Bond's Yard
15. Andrews Coaches
16. Mr Woodman's House
17. Infant School
18. Primary School

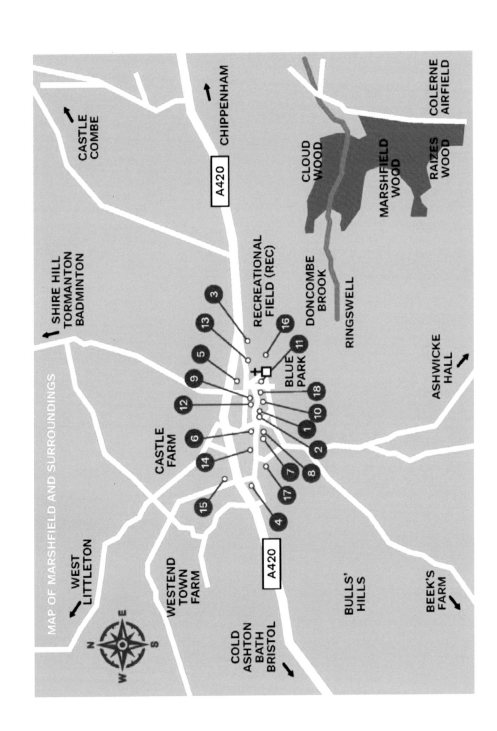

Contents

Introduction

I grew up in Marshfield, Gloucestershire close to where the three counties of Gloucestershire, Somerset and Wiltshire meet, as marked by the three shire stones. I had a postal address in Wiltshire, a Bath telephone number and I attended a secondary school in the suburbs of Bristol, so it always felt like 'Border Country'. I was born on 25th September 1949, post the Second World War, and as I found out later, sweet rationing was about to be cancelled and the UN had been formed. My early months were spent in a house, between Frank Bevan's Central Stores and the Post Office in the High Street, where the family had use of two rooms on the first floor, the kitchen and a garden. After about six months we moved to 3 Council Houses. The house had been constructed after the First World War and when we arrived had electricity, gas and running water. I shared the house with Mum, Dad and my elder twin sister Anita - we were born either side of midnight and the registrar insisted on the correct recording of our birthdays. I lived in the same house until going to university. It was a time of optimism after a period of global conflict in a 'protected' rural environment, which I was only able to fully appreciate after leaving Marshfield.

What follows are my own recollection of events. Whatever errors or omissions there may be are mine alone. I hope in some small way this short book will help you to think about your own lives, at whatever stage you may be, to encourage you to reach for your star and to be happy and contented.

Town History and Landmarks

With a population variously described as around 1,500 when I was growing up, Marshfield was and is a reasonable sized village or a town as I will explain shortly.

Marshfield is situated on the southern edge of the Cotswold Hills, some thirteen miles east of Bristol, nine miles north of Bath and nine miles west of Chippenham. There is a plaque just to the east of the butcher's shop in the High Street that records the town as being 103 miles from Hyde Park Corner. The original plaque was removed during the 1939-45 war, presumably in case of invasion and as part of a disinformation campaign.

Looking briefly back into the history of Marshfield, by the time of Norman Conquest the town was recorded as Meresfelde[1] (most likely from the Old English word March[2] which meant border) and was held by Queen Edith, the widow of Edward the Confessor, passing to Queen Matilda in 1075. Approximately a hundred years later Marshfield became part of the Abbey of Keynsham, where it remained for 400 years. It was the Abbot of Keynsham who in 1234 obtained the right to hold weekly markets plus a three day fair around St

---

[1] *Around Marshfield - Then and Now by Ian S Bishop*

[2] *Wikipedia reference to March (territory)*

Oswald's Day (5th August). Following the dissolution of the monasteries in 1548, the manor passed through several hands before being divided between the Goslett and Crispe families.

Samuel Rudder in 1789 described the town as:

'The town of Marshfield stands near the centre of the parish and consists chiefly of one street, nearly a mile long through which a turnpike road leads from London to Bristol. The business of making malt to supply the cities of Bath and Bristol was formerly very great here, for which the town is conveniently situated in a corn country; and though it has been for some time declining yet it is still pretty considerable. The market, which is but little frequented, except in the malting season, is held on a Tuesday and there are two fairs in the year, on 24th May and 24th October, for which privileges their charter was renewed in the reign of James I.'

Malting at its peak in the 15th and 16th centuries occupied no less than forty five houses, but by 1839 only sixteen maltsters were plying their trade. The years that followed saw a fall in prosperity and in 1865 a Field Gardens was established to provide gainful activity for the working classes who would otherwise have been needy. The lack of flowing water in the town prevented the establishment of mills, which would have allowed the development of other crafts and industries.

Today Marshfield is largely a commuter town for those working in Bristol, Bath and Chippenham, or further afield in London, Gloucester, etc. The proximity of the M4 motorway and good rail connections to the east, west and south at Chippenham, Bristol and Bath have been formative. It still retains strong links to agriculture and besides the shops and facilities to meet the needs of its inhabitants, there are several companies in the town involved in haulage, passenger coaches, boiler supply and ground works.

It would be impossible to talk about the town without talking about the weather. The climate in Marshfield was always seen to be rather extreme, particularly when it came to wind, rain and snow. The town is located on the southern end of the Cotswold Hills, and being rather exposed, it is not a surprise that power cuts occurred. Electricity supply, all above ground from the Midland Electricity Company, was variable and in any winter two or three power cuts could be expected so candles were always to hand. Rain comes predominantly from the south west, borne on winds from that direction. Snow, when it came, was exciting because besides the anticipation of 'school snow days' we were occasionally cut off from the outside world, with the lanes and byways that led into the town blocked. I recall the road down to Beek's Farm being filled to head height with snow, and men and tractors digging a way through.

Marshfield is well known for its long street through the town with practically every roof of a different pitch. The road used to be the main A420 until the bypass was built in the late 1960's. Prior to the bypass, traffic used to roar down the main street before slowing dramatically (or not as the case may be) at the double bend at the Lord Nelson. The town had, in my time, a good range of shops, pubs, banks and garages, though my father could remember more. Through my lifetime such businesses have decreased, but there are still the essential services that people need to ensure a vibrant community. Caroline Williams' 'Toll to Toll and Beyond', and Ian S Bishops' 'Around Marshfield-Then and Now' provide pictures of and information about many of the shops that I was familiar with in my youth and I will not repeat them here.

****

As a youngster I was always taught that Marshfield was a town and not a village, reflecting the fact that it had been a sizable community for hundreds of years. The town had a Mace and Constable's Stave[3]. The Mace was thought to have been presented to the town by Charles Goslett who became Lord of the Manor of 'Marshefeylde Magna (Great)' and 'Marshefeylde Parva

---

[3] *Toll to Toll and Beyond by Carolyn A Williams*

(Little)' upon the death of his father William in 1621. The Mace is a badge of office of the High Bailiff, who had duties in relation to the Almshouses and certain powers in the Manorial Court. Constables who attended the Bailiff held the Stave or Staff as a badge of office and were usually appointed annually by each 'Hundred'. (A Hundred is an area which is a subdivision of a county and Marshfield was in the upper division of the Thornbury Hundred).

The first meeting of the Parish Council took place in the National School Room on 4th December 1894 to elect councillors. There was a ruckus and a secret vote demanded, which was duly held with the original nominees largely elected. In recent years the Parish Council has met in the Tolzey Hall, which was built in 1690 for the town by John Goslett and his wife in the reign of William and Mary, and is adjacent to the Catherine Wheel pub. The building in its time has been a town house, lock-up, meeting room, charity school, public convenience and stored the town's fire engine! It was rebuilt in 1793.

Appreciating the history of the town was an important part of recognising how things could change over time and people's role in those changes

****

The Church of St Mary the Virgin is a dominant building in the town and located just off the Market Square. As in many parts of the West Country there were other places of worship (chapels) in the town and I can recall four. However, most people in the town when I lived there, if they expressed any religious beliefs, were likely to be Church of England and attended the Church.

Unlike the town, the history of the Church followed a different path. The town was the property of Keynsham Abbey in 1170, but records from Simon, Bishop of Worcester show that the Church had passed into the hands of Tewkesbury Abbey in 1125 *(3)*. In 1242 the Bishop of Worcester dedicated a newly built Church on the site of the present Church. After the dissolution of the monasteries, the gift of the benefice and the rector title was conferred by Queen Mary on the Warden and Fellows of New College Oxford in lieu of the property taken by Henry. In 1541 the Church passed to be under the jurisdiction of the Bishop of Gloucester, in 1836 to the combined bishopric of Gloucester, and Bristol and subsequently in 1847 to the Bishop of Bristol. The rector is now appointed alternately by New College Oxford and the Bishop of Bristol.

My early memories of Church were of Sunday School, the soft start into religion that most children experienced. Sunday School involved lots of colouring of items related to the religious year and I also recall collecting money for overseas missionary activities. Collections were made in paper mache canoes with a slit in the top where money could be entered, but not taken out.

The Sunday School also organised day trips to the seaside, often to Weston-super-Mare, although I recall Weymouth being a destination on at least one occasion. I cannot leave this section without mentioning the donkey rides at Weston-super-Mare and the invariable wind that blew across the sands. It was almost impossible to enjoy a meal on the sands without having a mouthful of sand. It left me with an inability to eat anything on beaches apart from perhaps the occasional ice cream.

The Primary School was a Church School and so to some extent a religious flavour to education was the norm. A conflict for me came when in my early teens I was selected to play for Marshfield cricket team and the timing of travel on a Sunday for away games could not accommodate attending Church services. I therefore fell out with religion until later when I attended The University of Birmingham and decided to be confirmed.

The Church Hall had been donated to the Church from Mr and Mrs Worthy Salmon *(3)* in 1932 (previously Bell Barn) and was a building situated around the back of Hay Street beyond what used to be England's Yard. It provided a social facility for the town with all sorts of societies and clubs able to meet there, including the Youth Club. It had a stage and curtains and I recall seeing several pantomimes performed there, all with local participants. I remember attending weekly Cub meetings at the Church Hall and a family wedding reception being held there when Auntie Nora and Uncle Dave were married. The Hall also provided a base for the Flower Show which was held annually.

****

The Almshouses were located at the western end of the town at the end of the High Street and on the opposite side of the road just before the water tower. They were built *(3)* between 1612 and 1619 by Ellis and Nicholas Crispe who were members of the large Crispe family who lived at the Mansion at Beeks. Ellis and Nicholas were sons of Thomas Crispe who, with his brother William, were successful and prosperous Bristol woollen merchants and maltsters. Ellis and Thomas moved to London in their early years and were members of the East India Company. They prospered as merchants in London and Bristol, and never forgot their origins in Marshfield. Thomas Crispe (a cousin) gave an acre of land to the town and Ellis and Nicholas erected the Almshouses for eight poor people of Marshfield. Various members of the Crispe family provided for the maintenance of the property, supported by a donation of £1,300 from Rev. Charles Parrott.

My connection with the Almshouses was that Nurse Whittard, who had been the District Nurse, lived in one of the houses in her later years and so along with Mum and Anita, I was a regular visitor. Nurse Whittard was a great friend of the Fuller family. Grampy Fuller also carried out maintenance on the clocktower and there is a photo of him on the scaffolding. Dad was also called upon to sort out several plumbing problems there and I joined him on more than one occasion.

****

Just opposite the grocery shop operated by Mr and Mrs Raven, and down from the Doctors Surgery at Bank House, past the entrance to the Royal British Legion Club, was no. 81 High Street. This property was owned at the time I lived in the town by Mr Rawlings who was the postman and the Town Crier in the Marshfield Mummers. The unusual feature of his house was that above the entrance to the house, on a plinth, was a Penny Farthing cycle. It had been used in earlier times to advertise a nearby cycle repair shop *(3)* and it remained there throughout my time in Marshfield and was always a notable landmark in the High Street. I think that it eventually rusted and became a safety hazard, so had to be removed.

****

In my youth there were four pubs in the town. The George, now converted to a house at the top of the town opposite the Almshouses, the Crown in the middle of the town, which was an old Coaching Inn and now under development, the Catherine Wheel and the Lord Nelson. The pubs now remaining in the town are all restaurants as well as pubs. My father could recall two more pubs in his lifetime - one in the Market Place called the Kings Arms and one just opposite the Catherine Wheel called the Angel. There was also the White Hart at the junction of Sheep Fair Lane and the High Street, which had closed much earlier. The number of pubs links to the original wealth of the town in providing barley for malting in the nearby cities of Bath and Bristol. The town prospered and several large houses, the Red House and the Maltings to name but two, were linked to wealthy merchants at this time.

Town Events and Entertainment

Many people know Marshfield through the Mummer's play that is performed on Boxing Day at three locations in the town. These 'paper boys', dressed up in costumes made of paper, perform their medieval play showing 'good triumphing over evil'. It was a must watch for me after Christmas Day, and in later years provided for good hospitality in the local pubs with some relatives coming back each year to join in the fun.

The Mummers were revived in Marshfield in 1932 by the Rev. Alford *(3)* who heard his gardener singing snatches from an Old St George's play which had been a Christmas tradition in the town, though sadly lost. It is performed by men of the town dressed as the following characters and led by the Town Crier:

Father Christmas

Little Man John

King William

Doctor Phoenix

Saucy Jack

Ten Penny Nit

Beelzebub

Performances last no more than 10 minutes and the 'paper boys' are led into a circle by the Town Crier and collections are made for charity. After the performances in my teens I retired to the local pubs with Dad. The pubs were heaving with people who had returned to the town, as well as locals and there was lot of bonhomie as well as beer being drunk. Returning home after such festivities Mum invariably had a lunch of cold meats, pickles, salad and mashed potato ready for us, after which the only sensible thing to do was to go to sleep for a couple of hours and wake up at one with the world.

****

Each year in August the Flower Show was held. It moved around the town over the years, but as I was growing up it was held in the field adjacent to the Church Hall, which is now occupied by houses. The facilities of the Church Hall could then be used to support the Show. The Show was preceded with a procession of tractors and vehicles through the town, dressed up by various organisations, and all vying for prizes to be awarded later. The main Show itself was housed in a large marquee (always hot and sticky) and was composed of exhibits of flowers, vegetables, cakes, preserves, sewing, knitting etc. Children were encouraged to enter items and these included miniature gardens and sketches or paintings of the town. I entered these categories with modest success over several years. Creating a whole garden in a box eighteen by twelve inches was always a challenge, especially when it came to selecting the grass. It was essential to avoid getting a patch with weeds and then, given its thickness, keeping it nice and green until the day of the show. Not quite the Chelsea Flower Show, but you get the idea!

Additionally, there were sporting activities at the Show including races, tug of war, skittling for a pig and a football competition, which was interesting on a field that was normally used for grazing cattle. I also recall a limited number of funfair sideshows being in place to gently while away the afternoon and the beer tent to keep all refreshed.

The Flower Show was a favourite country activity and one that drew all together and allowed everybody to show their skills and interests. It was a fun day with plenty of scope to compete with your friends and neighbours.

****

The men of the town usually had their preferred local pubs and Dad's was the Lord Nelson. Mum, along with most women of her generation, did not frequent the local pubs. The Lord Nelson was the closest to home and the landlady was Gwen Flower, a Cousin of Dad's on the Tiley side of his family. (Deviating for a moment, Reg

Flower, Gwen's husband, in addition to his publican duties also went to the fresh fruit and fish markets in Bristol and every week called around with our order of fish. This was delivered on a Tuesday, so fish and chips were the order of the day. The fish was 'whiting' and Mum used to cook it in homemade breadcrumbs - delicious! I can taste it now!)

My Grandfather Lewis also frequented the Lord Nelson and in later years had his chair just around the corner on the righthand side as you went into the pub. This was quite a precarious position until the bypass was built to the town. You were directly in line of vehicles coming west to east through the town as they rounded the first sharp bend of a double bend that the High Street takes at this point!

It was accepted that youths could visit pubs with fathers on the basis that no trouble was caused and this never happened because the threat of being banned from the pub was more than your life was worth! It was a practical arrangement in the days before off-licences and supermarkets widely sold alcohol. At the age therefore of probably no more than thirteen, but already six foot and looking older, I was taken to the pub by Dad and nobody 'batted an eyelid'. The progression in drinks started with brown ale and then moved to brown splits, a half of brown ale and half of bitter ale, before arriving at the promised land of bitter ale. I never did work out the thinking behind the progression. Brown ale was quite an acquired taste and slowed down the drinking though, so that may have been the logic.

Progressively the other men in the pub would recognise me and 'grunt' a hello as I arrived, but the ice breaker was being able to play cribbage and shove ha'penny. These were games that I played at home so I was able to acquit myself reasonably well from the word go and gain respect from the other players. The occasional win was like gold dust and whilst no money changed hands, a win was often followed by 'what are you drinking then young 'un'.

What was fascinating was seeing all the characters in the pub. Personas who in everyday life appeared in a certain way would be completely different in the pub, with no doubt the relaxation and looser tongue that came with consuming alcohol. It gave me an interesting perspective on how people fitted into the matrix of how the town functioned and operated. It also taught me that people sometimes have a different side to the one they usually portray, so not to make too many assumptions on a first meeting.

Besides alcohol, the pub was also my introduction to pickled eggs and onions. These were delicacies that were occasionally available and an acquired taste, of course to be followed by more ale.

Besides the Lord Nelson we occasionally visited the Crown and even less frequently the Catherine Wheel. I am not sure why these other pubs were not visited more often. The Catherine Wheel was run for many years by the same husband and wife team of Mr Hand who had married a Miss Legge, with all the obvious jokes and innuendos that you can imagine.

The Catherine Wheel was a substantial property on the opposite side of the street to the butcher's shop and had a skittle alley at the back of the pub. I can only recall using the alley once or twice.

****

Periodically the circus would come to town. I recall it being erected between the 'Barn', just above where we lived, and at the back of the small quarry which had been used to provide stone to build our house. The quarry was not surrounded by such large beech trees as now and the tennis courts (later to be built on) provided a southern boundary to the circus site. I also recall it being on the Recreation Field (Rec) on several occasions in later years. By the standards of Cirque du Soleil, these were modest affairs with rather older clowns who had seen many a laugh and exotic animals past their prime. Nevertheless, there was still the magic of the circus to soak up, although we only attended on a couple of occasions - perhaps the entry fees were too high. However, like all kids, we observed the moves being made by the travelling ensemble and sneaked the occasional glimpse under the canvas. It was a time before the impact of big spectaculars on television and it was the outside world coming to visit us in Marshfield, fuelling the imagination of all of us youngsters.

****

Fairs regularly came to the town attending the Flower Show on a small scale and on a larger scale as standalone entertainment. These latter fairs were usually held on the Rec and involved quite a set up time of three or four days before the events were ready. There was usually a build-up from a Thursday night with some attractions in place, with Friday and Saturday night being the main nights. Sundays were usually quiet with the travellers beginning to pack up and then moving off on the Monday to their next venue.

The attractions involved coconut shys, where we always questioned whether the coconuts were stuck on? As aspiring cricketers we fancied our throwing arm but there were few winners. Ping pong balls were thrown at arm's length to try and land them into goldfish bowls to win a goldfish. Shooting pellets from air guns at metal soldiers as they traversed your line of sight, and darts to stick a card and win a prize were also favourites. Dodgems, spinning seats, roundabouts and usually some device that flung you in the air at incredible angles were all available. Food such as hot dogs, candy floss and toffee apples (all highly nutritious no doubt and who was counting the calories!) were all on sale.

Financing the few days that the fair was in town was a challenge which involved raiding whatever savings had been accumulated and dropping into the conversation with any visiting relatives that the fair was in Marshfield. Mum and Dad either came to the fair and paid for some of the rides and entertainment, or as I grew older gave me an allowance to spend myself. I enjoyed the fun of the fair.

Today of course there are far fewer of these touring fun fairs. Maybe the way of life no longer appeals to travellers and the health and safety requirements are more stringent. Living in a rural town, the fun fairs brought a sense of otherworldliness to our lives and for that I was grateful. They provided an escape from everyday life in the town and provided fun and enjoyment to all the children.

****

I am old enough to recall a different type of fair in the town. Sheep fairs were held off the High Street in Back Lane, which could be accessed from Touching End Lane that ran adjacent to the grocer shop run by Mr. and Mrs. Raven. Fairs were held maybe once or twice a year but had stopped taking place by the time I was ten. The sheep were herded - with the occasional one escaping -

into pens which were made of gnarled and twisted wood to form the walls of the pen. As a young boy you could mingle with the farmers and buyers and touch the sheep through the pen, but always with the warning 'not to get your hand nipped' by the sheep who were sensing their destiny. It was a way of life that was dying out and had gone on for centuries, bringing buyers and sellers together and providing an opportunity to socialise and no doubt enjoy a pint or two of ale later.

Family

My childhood presented me with a good start in life as I had everything I needed, the opportunity to progress educationally and a family that was supportive. We lived in a rural community, which looking back was somewhat behind the development curve of the country, but that did not worry me. I was happy with school, the outdoor life and sport, and did not feel held back in any way. Mum and Dad loved me without necessarily showing that in a very demonstrable way because emotional displays then were perhaps not as usual as they are today.

I got on well with my sister Anita and at different times of our lives we have been drawn to each other for support. Being twins and having shared the same times, events and places, our views have been similarly shaped.

Mum and Dad had their challenges and held different views on a range of issues and that caused some upset for both Anita and I. When you are inside such a relationship it is sometimes difficult to figure out what is going on, but with time and perspective things fall into place.

As anybody who knows me would say, I am not a great pet lover, but when we were younger both Anita and I had pets. We had a cat and according to Mum we gave it a hard time, so either it ran away or met some other grisly fate. Anita had a pet rabbit called Bobtail which we looked after for a good number of years. It was kept in a hutch around by Dad's shed and, when it grew old and unwell, I went with Dad to the vets to see if it could be brought back to health, but unfortunately it had to be put down. I remember it being a sad day. Goldfish were usually won when the fair came to town by trying to get a bouncing ping pong ball into the very narrow top of a goldfish bowl. If you managed to win, you would be given the goldfish in a plastic bag containing water and then you had to buy a tank or bowl in which to accommodate the goldfish. Most of the time, despite the addition of 'water-weeds' and feeding as instructed, the goldfish never lasted more than a few months.

Bonfire night was a special night, as it was for the rest of the country, with Halloween having not been 'invented' yet. We used to have a bonfire in our back garden and the weeks leading up to the big night were taken up in collecting consumables to ensure a good blaze. Wood was in short supply as everybody else was seeking the same material, so trips to Marshfield Wood and other copses and hedgerows were made to collect fallen branches and boughs. The other main material for the fire were leaves, which were in good supply, but needed to be collected and dried out to avoid the whole fire becoming a smoking, steaming mass. The leaves were also useful in making a Guy Fawkes to go on the fire. I cannot recall whether we went collecting money 'Penny for the Guy'. Fireworks by today's standards were rather modest, but all the main types were available including sparklers, rockets, roman candles, Catherine wheels, bangers, etc. We used to buy a firework per week in the lead up to bonfire night and store them in tin boxes under our bed - very health and safety conscious! As we became older, after our own bonfire, we were taken around to the larger bonfire built on the Rec playing fields. Later again I went on my own. The bonfire was a much larger affair which was probably twenty foot high at its apex with a Guy Fawkes on the top.

Birthdays were always celebrated and given that Anita and I were twins with birthdays on consecutive days, Mum and Dad always ensured that we had separate parties. These were fun days. I recall birthdays when we were younger being with a few close friends and family at the house and sharing a cake, jelly and ice cream, Cadbury's chocolate fingers, nicely cut sandwiches and lemonade. As I grew older and through my teens, birthdays became more of a close family affair. Presents were always given and all the aunts and uncles used to send a card, usually with a small sum of money that could be safely placed in my National Savings Account.

Christmas was also a time of celebration. In the early days we had a Christmas tree adorned with simple decorations and small candles in holders clipped to the branches of the tree, which would not pass health and safety requirements today! Over time the candles were replaced by lights, but these were of the type that if one bulb went then the whole string of lights would not work. If two bulbs had blown, then there were lots of combinations to check to get the lights working again. General decorations around the house were simple ones involving lots of paper chains and the inevitable balloons. Christmas lunch involved the full range of Christmas fayre and Mum was in her element getting it all ready. In those days we had a large chicken with all the trimmings and plenty of vegetables from the garden. Dad always had problems 'dispatching' the chicken selected from those kept in the garden. I can picture now a rather bloodied chicken strung up by the legs against the washroom door, and finally being 'dispatched' by Uncle Ken who was visiting.

The main course was followed by Mum's home-made Christmas pudding and custard. We were all rather bloated after the meal, so tea was delayed somewhat into the evening, with mince pies and a Christmas cake to hand. As I guess for all children, we could not wait for presents, so the early part of Christmas morning was taken up with present opening. We always had a stocking - one of Dad's socks stuffed with oranges, nuts, a selection box, etc. I recall once when we were younger Bryan, an older Cousin, appeared as Father Christmas before the big day to wish us all a Happy Christmas and to encourage us to behave. These were magical times not to be forgotten.

****

Dad worked throughout my childhood in Marshfield. It never crossed my mind that he would be unemployed and after working for Grampy Fuller in the early days, he then went to work for and joined in a partnership with Bill Savage, who also worked in the town. Most of my memories come from the time Dad worked with Bill Savage, when Dad would work on the plumbing required and also any general building activities. The business was focussed on building new houses and carrying out larger extensions and repairs.

Mum during our earlier years was at home looking after the family. However there came a time when she embarked on part-time working. Initially, this was at Slaughterford Paper Mill, where she was involved in recycling waste board and paper. She found that work quite strenuous and decided to get a job in the stock room at Woolworths in Chippenham, where she had many happy years making several friends before retiring.

Mum and Dad's work provided a stable income coming into the house and I cannot recall us ever being short of money. That is not to say money was in limitless supply and both Mum and Dad were frugal with all expenditure, using their talents including gardening, sewing etc., to mitigate costs. Dad's normal working week included a Saturday morning and he usually used his bicycle if working locally, or perhaps his motorcycle, or car if the works van was not available. If possible, he would come home for lunch and would have a hot snack and cup of tea with his head buried in the newspaper, so there was not much conversation over lunchtimes. When Mum started work, Anita and I used to get his lunch and when Anita left school and went to work, I prepared his lunch. It was standard fayre such as baked beans on toast, toasted cheese, egg and bacon, etc., so not a demanding culinary range to master.

Undoubtedly Mum and Dad's work took a toll on them in their later years. They were hard working parents and that work ethic passed on to both Anita and I.

****

It would be incorrect to say that I became familiar with all aspects of plumbing from Dad. Inevitably though, when I accompanied him to his work I picked up quite a lot of information. Dad could manage lead pipe work, as well as wider bore copper pipe, and I therefore learned how to install and repair such systems. Lead piping was decreasing as a preferred piping option and copper installations were in the ascendancy. However that left a lot of legacy systems in place that needed repairing or extending. One case in point was at the Old Vicarage, where I think Dad was the only person in the town that knew where the pipework ran. By accompanying him in his work, I met different people, saw other homes, as well as learning a little about the trade. I still have Dad's old wooden tools for working in lead, which I am sure are now old enough to be in a museum.

The widespread advent of central heating systems was a major innovation which Dad had to master. He was for using gravity-based systems (relying on hot water rising and cold water falling under gravity) and would only look to install an electric pump if absolutely required. The heating source could be either coal, oil or gas and the advent of central heating systems lead to quite an expansion of work for Dad.

As Dad was one of only two plumbers in the town (the other being Jack Walters) there were the inevitable emergency knocks at the front door, particularly through some of the harsh winters that Marshfield seemed to endure. Dad always responded, even though that meant working some odd hours into the night and it was fun to join him on such occasions.

My knowledge even today of general household plumbing comes from that time with Dad, so thank you to him for those experiences.

****

Whilst growing up, I gradually realised that I had a speech impediment - a stutter - and had difficultly pronouncing words especially those beginning with 'U' or 'Y'. I am not sure if Mum and Dad ever took any advice on how the stutter might be improved upon or eradicated. Today I am sure some measures would have been taken, albeit I know from others how difficult it can be to eliminate a stutter. It was occasionally terrifying and caused me often not to join in conversations for fear of making a fool of myself. Telephones were a nightmare and I only mastered them when I went away to university. Without any support - it was never talked about at home - I grew out of stuttering and managed techniques to avoid starting sentences with either a 'U' or a 'Y'. What helped me, as Head Boy at School, was the occasion I had to give a vote of thanks to the main speaker on Speech Day. I devised the speech myself, avoiding those dreaded 'U's' and 'Y's', and whilst I was terrified, I completed the speech without mishap. As is frequently the case after such an ordeal, my confidence was raised and it helped me to break free. Later in life the stuttering decreased as a problem and only reappears now when I am very tired or had a few too many drinks! It is interesting that I ended up working for Unilever, a company whose name begins with 'U'!

****

In tracing back my family history in recent years, it turns out that my forebearers were quite local to Marshfield. Both of my Grandfathers lived in the town. Unfortunately both Grandmothers died before I was born. My Great Grandfather was still alive when I was younger and lived in the town. Mum and Dad lived their lives (other than the war years and going into service) in Marshfield. Going back further, Dad's mother was a Tiley, a family who were well established in the town. Dad's father's history can be traced back to Alderley in Gloucestershire in the mid 1700's. On Mum's side of the family, the Fuller family originally came from around Shepton Mallet and the Short family from close to Berkeley.

Mum was one of five siblings (four surviving) and Dad was one of ten siblings (nine surviving), so I had a ready-made group of friends and relations as cousins were born. Most of the aunts and uncles had moved out of Marshfield to the suburbs of Bristol, with two in Bath and one in Chippenham. Only Mum and Dad and Uncle Percy were 'hard core' Marshfield residents. Grampy Lewis lived next door to us at No 4. Chippenham Road and had married Aunty Janet, as we called her, following the death of Kathleen his first wife. Aunty Janet also died before I left for university. Grampy Fuller stayed in Rose Cottage, his family home, and after Mum's marriage to Dad, Nelly, Mum's sister, moved in to look after him with her son Bryan. She stayed until she married Ron Andrews and then moved to Batheaston to run a guest house. At that time, Mum's brother Uncle Percy and his family moved into Rose Cottage.

The family members who had moved away from Marshfield loved to come back to the town and surrounding villages to visit the local pubs. A lot of them had purchased motor cars and were seen to be doing well and moving ahead. Mum was anxious to 'move under the hill', but Dad clearly was not and this led to a lot of discussions over many years.

The regularity of family visits placed a hospitality burden on Mum, which occasionally led to some discontent.

When Grampy Lewis lost Aunty Janet, Mum agreed to step into the breach to provide him with food, wash his laundry and clean the house. Eventually this was reduced to providing him with meals, with the other aunts taking up the laundry and cleaning duties.

One thing that we did with the wider family was go on holiday with them. I did not go on holiday (for a week) until I was about ten years old and I recall a range of holidays with Aunty Glad, her family, and Auntie Dor and Uncle Spike. These holidays were around the south coast to Dorset, Devon and Cornwall. We either stayed in caravans or apartments and prayed for fine weather. I enjoyed swimming in the sea, having time on the beach, seeing the sights and collecting badges from the places I had been. The badges were then sewn or stuck onto my duffle bag. Before we had a motor car, we relied upon trains to get to locations. Breakfast and lunch were simple affairs, but in the evenings fish and chips and steak and chips were on the menu – wonderful! A few pints were drunk by the men in the group and the ladies had Babycham or port and lemonade, with the children receiving their quota of lemonade and crisps. I recall during most holidays attending shows, which ran at the seaside locations where we stayed. These were variety shows with the occasional star name from the television, but consisted mainly of journeymen entertainers.

I remember on one of these holidays, going out into Weymouth Bay fishing for mackerel. There were so many to pull into the boat and I was overjoyed that we could take some home and cook them that evening for dinner.

I also recall going on holiday with Bill Savage and his family on a couple of occasions to Butlin Camps at Minehead and Clacton. The latter was in 1966 when England won the World Cup and we were in transit to Clacton - definitely an own goal. Butlins at that time was in the 'Hi de Hi' post-war mode, with mass entertainment, communal eating and lavish (we thought) evening entertainment.

It was natural to form closer relationships with some cousins than others, either as we saw more of them, or we were closer in age. I guess that my closest cousin was Michael. I had grown up with him in Marshfield and we went to the same secondary school, where he was only one year behind me. We shared a close interest in sport and went on holiday together in our late teens. Bryan was a little older and, as you will recall when you are younger, a few years makes a big difference. Other boys in the family - Nigel and Tim were younger and Aunty Peg's three boys - Derek, Paul, and Rob, we did not see that often. The female cousins were somewhat remote to me, although quite close to Anita. It was just the way at that age.

A family feature for a good number of years, particularly before becoming a teenager, were the regular family picnics to Cloud Wood and Marshfield Wood on the banks of Doncombe Brook. In some years there would be maybe up to twelve of us, with some walking to the venue, which was quite a hike, and others going in cars. All necessary food and gear had to be transported, including blankets and a primus stove run on paraffin (prior to camping gas stoves) so that everybody had to play a part. The walk was rewarded by seeing various wildflowers on the way, most commonly primroses and blue bells. It was usually too early for the crab apples or blackberries, but wild strawberries could be found.

The family picnics were not without their tensions, but given the wide range of participants I guess that is not surprising. After all it was a 'bit of a family do'.

Given my familiarity with the woods, I was in my element running on ahead and indicating to all the salient features as we went. The final approach to the brook was a steep descent covered in molehills, so there was always a discussion about having the picnic on the top of the descent or down by the brook. The brook provided a range of distractions, including various small fish and water life such as dragonflies, water boatman, tadpoles, the occasional frog etc. Watercress grew in the stream and there was usually a discussion about whether it would be healthy to eat, remembering that the Ringswell water treatment plant was upstream! We also built dams across the stream.

The other distraction was the defensive pillbox left over from WW2. We were not too far from RAF Colerne and the pillbox was well placed, so you could imagine playing out roles defending the homeland to the death.

The food was typical 1950/60's picnic food and rather plain by today's standards, but eating outdoors seemed to swell everybody's appetite. All food was eaten which meant that we did not have to carry any back home! A tea brew was quickly organised for the adults with lemonade for the kids. Occasionally sausages were cooked and baked beans warmed on the stoves.

The other feature of the picnics were rabbits. In Mum and Dad's youth, rabbits contributed to most local family diets but rabbits had been decimated by myxomatosis since 1953. By the time of our picnics, rabbits were making a comeback and they could be seen around the fields and hedgerows.

Other family gatherings during this period were baptisms and weddings. I particularly recall the weddings of Cousins Brenda and Lynda, and of Aunty Nora. We only attended baptisms if Mum or Dad were invited as a godparent.

At one of the family weddings, it was my first occasion to wear long trousers. I was wearing a suit that Cousin Bryan had grown out of, which was a light green and brown check, and I wore brown shoes. I felt a million dollars and all grown up!

****

One event which involved my Uncles Harold and Fred was when I was invited over to an Open Day at the Filton Aerodrome factory where they both worked. Fred was a technician and Harold was a draughtsman. The day was important to me as it introduced me to technology first- hand and further stimulated an interest in science and technology. I particularly remember the soft blue putty that bounced which Uncle Fred gave me a free sample of. There was quite a lot going on in and around Bristol at that time in terms of aeronautical engineering. It was not so long after the Blue Streak missile had been launched, the Lightening Fighter was in service and Concorde was being developed and manufactured. There was therefore plenty to grasp a young boy's attention.

****

When we were much younger, Mum took both Anita and I to see Nurse Whittard and Great Grampy Fuller. Great Grampy, Arthur Fuller, worked as a blacksmith at the forge in the High Street by Bond's Yard, and we saw him in his house (115 High Street) almost opposite the forge. My abiding memory when seeing him was that he always gave us a blood orange, saying that it was extremely healthy. He died in 1958, having been born in 1871 and was a connection to the years before the First Boer War.

Nurse Whittard had been the district nurse in her working life. She had not married and retired to live in the Almshouses. She had come to the town and was befriended by Mum's mother, Violet, and lived for some time in Rose Cottage, 96 High Street. She had been exceedingly kind to Mum throughout her life and when Violet died, the strong bond between them was reinforced. As children we went to see Nurse Whittard at the Almshouses and she was generous in giving us books and a mug which I still have. I recall in her old age she became quite short and wore a knitted hat.

Anita and I were never able to enjoy being with a Grandmother or indeed a Great Grandmother, as they had died before we were born. Both Grandfathers and a Great Grandfather were still alive and we were able to share our childhood with them. I often think about our two Grandmothers and what they could have added to our upbringing.

****

Having spent my first six months in a small property on the High Street between Bevan's Grocery Shop and the Post Office, a Council House later renamed Chippenham Road, became available at No. 3, next door to Grampy Lewis. Mum and Dad managed to secure the move because of Dad's war service and the unexpected arrival of twins (Mum had only been told to expect twins late on in her pregnancy). The house had been built after the First World War and was originally serviced with water from a well. By the time of our arrival the house had gas, electricity, and water from the mains. Years later, Dad and I capped off the well that serviced our house to make it secure.

****

The house had three rooms, plus a hallway on the ground floor and an outside toilet. The room which housed the kitchen was a single-story lean-to made of wood and asbestos sheeting. Dad had constructed it upon moving into the house, as originally the kitchen and daily living area were all in one. Besides being used as a kitchen, it became our bathroom when we had our weekly bath in a tin bath on Friday evenings. In order to save heating up too much water, which had to be heated in a standalone gas boiler, there was an order of bathing with Anita first, then me, then Mum and then Dad, with water topped up as we progressed. It does not sound very hygienic by today's standards, but together with vigorous washing every other day of the week it kept us healthy. Palmolive soap was used for personal washing and it was only in later years that shampoo was used with a little deodorant. Given the obvious state of undress and confusion surrounding Friday nights, any visitors that happened to drop in that night were not welcome! Drying your hair was conducted near the fire in my early years and we were not allowed to go anywhere until it was thoroughly dried. Eventually a hairdryer appeared, but Mum felt it was a new-fangled thing and thought it much better to dry your hair by the fire. The hair dryer did eventually gain acceptance and allowed us to avoid queuing to dry our hair by the fire.

****

Upstairs in the house were three bedrooms leading off a landing. At the front of the house were Anita's and Mum and Dad's bedrooms with mine at the rear of the house. There was initially no central heating in the house, with the main fire being in the living room. Other rooms had a fireplace that could be sealed off when not in use and heating was by burning coal. Coal was delivered in a one tonne lot in early Autumn and stored in the shed adjacent to the house. During the Winter the fire was kept in overnight by stacking up the fire with fine coal dust that had been wetted ('slack') and the fire would still be alight in the morning. This kept the main room warm, but in other rooms it was not unusual to have frost and ice on the inside of windows, which did not clear during the day. A small electric fire was available to move around the house to warm up rooms quickly. When the bathroom was eventually built there was an electric fire on the wall that radiated heat when switched on. It was like being in the tropics compared to the normal temperatures around the house during the Winter.

Washing of clothes was a major activity. The house had been originally designed with a single-story wash house attached to the back of the house, where all the activity of washing and drying would have occurred. By the time we had moved into the house, the boiler connected to gas was brought into the lean-to building that Dad had constructed and a mangle operated to squeeze out the clothes once they had been boil-washed. The mangle was hand operated and as children we were warned to keep well clear. Starch, brand name Robin, was applied to shirts and other items that needed to be stiffened and the washing line was then festooned with drying clothes, bedding etc. During Winter drying of clothes was a major problem and to get through the kitchen required passing through a maze of items hung up to dry. There then followed the job of ironing and, as most things were ironed, this was a lot of work with a heavy iron. I recall Mum spending probably two days of the week washing and ironing clothes, and everything had to be spotless.

The house was on a sizable plot, which at the rear of the house provided a cultivated area for vegetables, gooseberry and blackcurrant fruit bushes. Chickens were also kept there when I was younger. I comment elsewhere on gardening, and Dad with increasing help from me, worked the garden to maximise the range and yield of vegetables and fruit. At the front of the house was a pathway and lawn with a hedge on one side separating us from Mr and Mrs Fields at No. 2. On the other side it was more open because originally that had led to the well which serviced several houses.

The outside toilet was a place to visit at speed, particularly during the Winter. There was no heating that I can recall, although how the water did not freeze I am not sure. The combination of Izal toilet paper, in tight rolls with green wrappers, was a far stretch from the pampered soft Andrex adverts of today.

The Council finally decreed that things had to change and the lean-to and outside toilet were replaced with a kitchen built on the ground floor and a bathroom upstairs. It was the height of luxury and was transformational as activities in the kitchen progressively changed with the purchase of a refrigerator, electric kettle, toaster, washing machine (always a top loader as Mum could not countenance a side loader) and eventually a tumble drier. Carpet cleaning also changed with the purchase of a Hoover to replace the push-along carpet sweeper.

It was somewhat ironic that Dad, being a plumber, took quite a time before he installed a central heating system which also provided hot water in our house. The wider family generally had invested in Baxi fires, which were coal fires that could heat a room but also direct the fire to heat water and a limited number of radiators. The system involved some trade-offs and forethought was required if you wanted hot water and hot radiators, let alone a hot room. This led to numerous 'discussions' between Mum and Dad about the veracity of the system. The efficiency of the system was compounded by Dad's insistence that the central heating of about four radiators, should work on gravity alone and not be reliant on pumps that could fail. Unfortunately, this did not make for the speediest of responses in the central heating system.

****

Mum was an excellent cook, but then I guess many children say that about their mother's cooking. It is one of the most evocative memories we all hold. By today's standards her cooking would probably be described as homely. It was hugely important to her that we had sufficient on our plates, that we left clean plates, and enjoyed our meals. Dad grew most of the vegetables that we needed, with only potatoes, apples and pears brought in for the winter months. Eggs were laid in the early days by the chickens we kept at the back of the house, but in later years were obtained from Hitchcock's Farm along the Tormarton Road. Eggs were stored in times of plenty in silica gel, which made the shells non-porous to gases, and preserved them for the Winter. Root vegetables (carrots, beetroot etc.) were stored in a sand pit allowing relatively easy access in the winter when frosts made the soil impenetrable. Bread was obtained daily, or every other day, from Hammond's the bakery in the town. Meat was purchased from Ford's the butchers where I worked as a butcher's boy for some years, but also via the Co-op delivery. This latter service was once a week from Bath and was an early form of home-delivery. You ordered your requirements for the following week (largely dry and canned foods, bacon and butter etc.) at the time of your delivery in the current week. There was a dividend that could be collected and cashed in at Christmas and this later migrated to 'green shield stamps' that were collected and used in a similar way at Christmas time. Milk was delivered daily, except on Sunday, by the Co-op and fish was brought once a week, on a Tuesday, by Mr Flower.

Before fridges and freezers, items were stored in the pantry and some perishable goods were stored in a meshed cupboard to protect them from flies. The system worked well, except in the height of Summer when items could become a 'little ripe'. Organising consumption before things got out of hand was therefore important.

Mum cooked on a gas stove with a single oven and grill. Water was boiled initially on the stove, or in the boiler for washing, before the arrival of an electric kettle and hot water on tap. Toast was made on the fire and then under the gas grill before the advent of the electric toaster. I can recall making toast on a toasting fork held close to the fire in the living room, where it was important to get your timing right to avoid total incineration!

Mum was prolific in making cakes, especially the small sultana cakes made several times a week and cooked directly in the tin, with the best part being the 'overhang'. Either a fruit cake or a victoria sponge cake was made every week.

Ice cream was never eaten at home until we purchased a freezer in my teens. The 'ice cream man' would come around periodically in his van and then there was the rush to get there before he pulled away. In those days you purchased a rectangle of Wall's ice cream in a cornet or wafer, or an iced lolly. We were not allowed to have ice creams every time the van called, so imagine my delight today in having ice cream in my freezer, particularly with the more recent introduction of Marshfield ice cream.

Savoury snacks were not widely available and crisps were not eaten at home. As described later, we had crisps and a bottle of pop when we went to the pub with aunts and uncles.

Sweet snacks were available, but I would say in my early years these were traditional children's boiled or chewy sweets, with not many chocolate coated bars being available. Biscuits were, by today's standards, rather plain. In my teenage years this changed as chocolate bars became more widely available - my favourite at the time being the Lion bar.

The fish and chip van from Colerne came around, and very occasionally in my teenage years we indulged in some chips on a weekend night. High living indeed!

***

There were discussions at home about money, not in the sense of there not being enough, although things must have been tight on occasions, but rather about discretion in spending money. We are talking here before the advent of the joint bank account. Both Mum and Dad were thrifty and ingenious at making things at home, particularly Mum who knitted, sewed, darned and repaired all manner of items of clothing. Nobody ever went out looking scruffy. When Mum returned to part time work she had an income that she could use at her discretion.

During my teenage years I undertook a range of jobs to supplement my pocket money. I was a butcher's boy for Mr Ford on Saturday mornings and just able to make it to Saturday afternoon football during the season. I rode one of those bicycles with a basket at the front and no gears, so besides getting to know my way around the town I became very fit. Unfortunately, the job brought me into conflict with the School as I was no longer available for the School football and cricket teams and I was wheeled into the Head's study for a reprimand. There is a comment for one year in my School report on the matter. However, after leaving the butcher's round and returning to Saturday morning sport the relationship with School settled down again. Besides my Saturday morning wage, which was fifteen shillings at the outset (seventy five pence in today's money), Mr Ford occasionally offered some lamb's breast for Mum to cook. Doug Grey and Ron Whale also worked in the shop, as well as Mrs Ford. They had daughters Annette (who married Rodney Bond) and Sally, and they went to a private school in Bath. I also delivered papers for Mrs Buoy (no relation to Mr Buoy mentioned elsewhere) when regulars were off on holiday or ill. For one summer vacation I worked at Brain's Faggot and Pie factory down from the common at Mangotsfield. It was quite an experience as this was my first 'official' job with a payslip and tax to pay, which I then had to reclaim. It was an education working on the line with all the 'ladies' and then in the cold store at minus 20 degrees (30 minutes inside with a donkey-jacket on and 10 minutes out). Even Marshfield winters seemed warm after that experience.

I was fortunate to be able to work on the Marshfield bypass in the late 1960's under the tutelage of Mr Frost. I also at that time undertook some road sweeping around the town and learnt the art of pushing a brush for eight hours a day without going crazy. Tom Buoy was also working with the Council at that time and I worked alongside him.

Anita left school to join the civil service after her 'O' levels and was earning some money herself. I also recall she worked at the Crown at Tolldown, as a barmaid, on Saturday nights in her late teens.

As children we were encouraged to save money in the Post Office National Savings Account, which involved putting in small sums and seemingly never taking any money out. When Premium Bonds came along in 1956, we obtained a few pounds worth expecting large cash prizes. If we had known the odds of winning we would not have been so expectant.

I opened my first bank account with the National Westminster bank which was located just below the Catherine Wheel pub. I went to the bank, when I was in my later teens, in expectation of going to university and needing a bank account. I was accompanied by Mum and Grampy Fuller (he held an account at National Westminster bank) and was interviewed by the Bank Manager, who agreed that I could open an account and requested a sample signature from me. Walking out of the bank I somehow felt that I had gone up one notch on the pole of life.

Mum and Dad were very generous in funding me to go to the University of Birmingham. At the time, academic fees were paid by the county and a living allowance was means tested. It meant that only about half of the living allowance was paid by the county and the other half paid by the family. It was a significant amount and they paid it willingly. As I found out when I arrived at university, other students had not been so fortunate.

****

It is hard to recall a world in which the ubiquitous photograph taking of today, anywhere at any time on a smart phone, was not available and how much rarer photographs were during my youth. Mum and Dad had a set of photographs for their wedding and other occasions were marked by photographs being taken. The official school photographs mapped progress through school and other than that there was the occasional and rather small, three inches square, print that emerged. In the early days all photographs were black and white. When colour photographs became available they were more expensive and faded somewhat badly in the sunlight, although in this aspect they improved over time. From Mum and Dad I received a Kodak camera following my Eleven Plus results. After my GCSE results, I was given an upgraded Single Lens Reflex (SLR) camera and my photography skills improved.

It is interesting looking back at Mum and Dad's photo collection, as well as my own photos from this time, and understand how they capture the times in which they were taken. I wonder in this digital age whether and how people will enjoy their memories from their photographs?

****

Growing up in Marshfield it was natural to develop a deep understanding of the seasons. Before the advent of television, and even afterwards, it was normal to spend most free time after completing any homework outside of the house, either playing sport, gardening or exploring the countryside. An understanding of the seasons and whether you were likely to be, for example, rained upon or even snowed upon, was useful. Marshfield displayed the full force of the seasons being quite exposed and it was often windy and a few degrees lower in temperature compared to Bath or Bristol. I do however remember glorious sunny days and lounging on the paving stones in the High Street when it was too hot to sit on them.

The Seasons were a critical part of gardening, as was the cycle in which things were to be planted, tended and harvested. Dad had me gardening from quite an early age both in the vegetable patch at the rear of the house and out at 'Field Gardens', where we had an allotment that was dedicated to potatoes and greens. Today I still clearly remember the order in which to grow vegetables and hope to pass that on to coming generations. I really enjoy growing vegetables. For Mum and Dad it was a necessity, which for me is not the case. Rather it is about connecting to a simpler life - The Good Life as Richard Briars and Felicity Kendal would express it.

****

Mum and Dad always ordered and read the Daily and Sunday Mirror. Dad used to read the newspaper from cover to cover and progressively I took up the habit of reading the paper to keep abreast of national and international developments. However, it became clear that some of the articles in the paper were somewhat biased and did not offer the challenge I was looking for. In my mid-teens I therefore decided that I wanted to purchase the Sunday Times and the Scientific American magazine that came once a month. I paid for these out of my earnings from my jobs, pocket money, gifts and savings. I recall that the Sunday Times used to take me most of the week to read as it was heavy going in parts and there were so many supplements and magazines to study. Dad did not ever look at the Times and resolutely stuck to the Mirror. Scientific American was a direct response to my growing interest in science and technology. The space race was underway and as well as articles on space, there was also a lot of coverage of biotech subjects following Watson and Crick's announcement on the double helix model of DNA in 1953. The latter articles had a direct effect on my choice of subject as I progressed to university.

We did not have a bookcase downstairs, but I recall having a small bookcase in my bedroom. I read my schoolbooks very thoroughly and amassed a small technical library from the prizes that I obtained at school. In my teenage years, I cannot recall reading widely literature and the arts. In my earlier years, I had many annuals and the classic children's books which I still have, but this did not blossom into a wide breadth of reading material. My reading was focused on sport, geography, nature, science and technology, which probably explains my performance today at Trivial Pursuit!

****

As for all children, the fun and freedom of being able to move under your own power, and of course be released from family ties, was empowering. I therefore progressed from tricycle and scooter to bicycle and was able to roam widely in and around the town. Journeys were planned with friends that involved expeditions to far flung places, which were probably no further than four miles from the town, but the sense of exploration was palpable, if somewhat tiring, as Marshfield was hilly. The occasional puncture slowed me down, but learning how to mend punctures was all part of being mobile. The bike was well looked after, being cleaned down and oil applied as required. I never had more than a three-speed bicycle, although derailleur gears were becoming available and some boys had them on their bikes, which meant that I had to pedal faster to keep up! An innovation that most boys went in for was to attach a piece of stiff card or plastic to the frame of the bicycle and have it interact with the spokes on the rear wheel. As the rear wheel went around the card was distorted by a spoke but flicked back into position as the next spoke arrived, producing a clicking sound. At speed, the effect simulated the noise of a low powered motorcycle, so we were all pretending that we had engines on our bicycles. The cardboard eventually either suffered from fatigue or got wet, then had to be abandoned and replaced.

Buses were the means to move between Marshfield and the towns of Chippenham, Bath and Bristol that we visited primarily for shopping. When a family car was purchased some of the shopping visits on the bus were replaced by visits in the car.

As well as the bus trips there were also coach trips, either with Ryan's Bluebird coaches, which operated out of premises just opposite the butcher's shop, or with Andrew's coaches which were parked in premises along Castle Farm Lane.

In the early days Dad had his push bike and a BSA (Birmingham Small Arms) 'Bantam' motorcycle. I had my tricycle and then my bicycle and apart from that the family either relied upon buses or other family members who by that time had acquired cars. We would all squash in and go out, usually to a local pub for crisps and a bottle of lemonade for us kids. On 1st August 1963, Dad bought his first car for £411, a grey Morris Minor 1000, with the help of Mum's friend Phyllis' husband, Norman Treaby. The car was a revelation and had indicators on either side that came up when you were turning left or right. As we found out, they were quite prone to pedestrians bending them, but hey we thought we were the 'bee's knees'. Suddenly holidays were possible, as well as visits to country houses and other sites. I passed my driving test at the first attempt when I was 17 going on 18, using an instructor's car. I was then allowed to use Dad's car on occasions and to drive the family when we were all together. Even when we had the car, longer trips were still taken by coach or very occasionally by train, primarily for holidays.

****

My earliest memory of having my haircut was at Mr Woodham's at Little End, the last house on the left-hand side as you left the town. Arriving at what was a creosoted garden shed in Mr Woodham's garden, you joined the queue of men and boys who were submitting themselves to a 'one size fits all' haircut. The haircut was executed using manual clippers and scissors to achieve the required shortness on the back and sides, and some length on the top. Of course there was the mandatory slick of Brylcreem that ensured nothing was left sticking out or could be moved by even the strongest of Marshfield winds.

Eventually, Mr Woodham retired and I then changed to Mr (Charlie) Chivers, who had a barber's shop just above the butcher' shop. Charlie was a man of many talents, being the local postman and a tobacconist, as well as a barber. It was during my attendance at Charlie's that the innovation of longer hair and the square cut to the back of the neck came into fashion - even in Marshfield. The use of Brylcreem persisted until well into my teens and was then abandoned to achieve the volume and bounce that was required.

****

A rite of passage for any boy is having your first shave and marks the transition from boyhood to manhood. Dad always used to shave at the kitchen sink because the upstairs bathroom was in use by the rest of the family. He used a safety razor and a stick of solid shaving soap with a soft bristled stubby 'badger' brush. The brush was wetted and then rubbed onto the stick to generate a soapy lather, which was then applied generously to the chin and sides of the face. The safety razor was then loaded with a fresh blade, if required, with the new blade being carefully handled to avoid cuts on the fingers. Then shaving could commence, but with caution as incorrect angles and less than taut skin meant you could end up being cut quite badly. It was not unusual to end up after shaving with several pieces of paper attached to the skin, where the blood came from, only to find that the bleed would recommence when the paper was removed.

My first shave occurred, which was perhaps not a wise choice, before a wedding we were attending - I cannot recall if it was either Cousin Brenda's, Lynda's or Auntie Nora's. Inevitably, even under close instruction from Dad, there were some whiskers left in position and some cuts to show for my endeavours. I did however feel good about it and joined a few others at the wedding in a similar condition.

****

We always had a radio in the house, one of those old valve-based ones that heat up to quite a high temperature if you leave them on some time. My abiding memory of the radio is listening to Forces Favourites in the run up to Sunday lunch and shelling peas or slicing beans just outside of the back door. For Mum and Dad, I knew, having both been through the war, this programme was a time to chill out before the main meal of the week, after which Dad would invariably take an hour's snooze upstairs.

Televisions were mass produced during the 1950s and we acquired our first set in this period. Uncles Fred and

Stan had the contacts, so we purchased an Echo black and white set, which had a picture about fifteen inches square. The picture was not that sharp and, depending on the atmospherics, had some snow effects across the screen. Nevertheless, it was a game changer and suddenly the world opened beyond just the town and the radio. The Echo gave way to a range of sets, with coloured pictures coming along and the first transatlantic live transmission in 1962, via the Telstar satellite to Goonhilly in Cornwall, was a milestone in international news coverage.

We acquired a television too late to view the early children's programmes like Muffin the Mule etc., but programmes such as Blue Peter, Sooty and Sweep and Basil Brush were watched with pleasure. As we grew up, Billy Cotton's Big Band Sound was available, as well as Russ Conway, Petula Clark, Black and White Minstrels (not appropriate today), Crackerjack and Sunday Night at the London Palladium were all favourites.

In the house I recall an old record player which played '78's' and had a needle which was placed carefully on the record, having wound up the turntable with a handle. This was replaced with a much newer electric model, which I think was a present to Anita, and I recall it being red and white and placed on four legs in the corner of the room. It could handle Long Playing (LP) and Extended Playing (EP) records, as well as Singles.

The old records could not be played on this record player, but all the modern records and associated performers could. I received a present of a Grundig portable radio that allowed me to listen to the radio in my bedroom or outside of the house.

I did not go to the cinema until I was taken with Mum, Dad and Anita with Uncle Fred and Auntie Glad to watch 'The Sound of Music' in Bristol. It was a night to remember given Julie Andrews' performance in the film, but also because we went to a Bernie Inn and had chicken in the basket. I thought we had hit the good life. From then, I went occasionally to the cinema, usually in Bath, after going swimming and having a portion of chips from Evans fish and chip shop in Abbeygate Street. I recall seeing 'Summer Holiday' with Cliff Richards, as well as a couple of James Bond movies.

We never had a telephone in the house until after I went to university and the nearest telephone was next to the post office in the High Street. Life was organised around either the regularity of doing things - every week or month, on a surprise basis or based on a written communication, which was more prevalent than today. The surprise element led to some tensions - I mentioned in the early days that Friday evenings were bathing night, so visitors were not particularly welcome at that time. Additionally, if people just dropped by to go out there was the rush to get ready to join them, which also caused some angst on occasions. Nevertheless, life was more local and less just in-time than today.

****

As I have mentioned elsewhere, Mum was very competent at knitting, sewing and needlework. She had a Singer sewing machine driven by a handle and was able to create all sorts of clothes. For me, this meant that she made jumpers, cardigans, socks (short and long woollen ones) and gloves in the early days. Shirts, trousers, coats, topcoats, mackintoshes, pyjamas and underwear etc., all had to be purchased, mainly from Marks and Spencer. Shoes were usually purchased from Clark's in Bath or Bristol. My school uniform for secondary school was purchased from Horne Brothers in Bristol, at what Mum considered were high prices.

As I grew-up I was keen to wear mass produced items to match my peers and so gradually the home produced clothes decreased, but I recall Mum still knitting quite complicated cricket and other jumpers for me in my mid-teens. Fashion frankly was not top of the agenda for a boy growing up in Marshfield. Jeans had arrived, but I did not have a pair until my late teens. I also recall buying shoes with longer chiselled points and then ones with a significant point (commonly called winkle pickers). Other shoes were made of suede leather and had to be brushed carefully to remove dust and dirt.

Ties varied from narrow and plain, to wide and large flowery ones - we were heading towards Woodstock and the era of Flower Power!

****

Dr Eastes ran his surgery out of a large house, called Bank House on the opposite side of the High Street to the Malting House and just up from the entrance to the Royal British Legion Hall. His wife, Zeta Eastes, had worked in the practice previously, but not a lot during my time growing up. Anita and I were quite an item in the town because twins were far more unusual in those days compared to today with in vitro fertilisation being available. My encounters with doctors were not frequent, although when I was quite young I had my tonsils and adenoids removed at Bath Royal United hospital. I recall either being taken down or picked up by Dad in a works van and receiving ice cream at some stage. A full recovery was made.

The waiting room for the doctor was the large hallway of the house, with chairs placed around the walls. There was no appointment system, so it was first come first served and the wait was always somewhat terrifying. Besides conducting an examination, Dr Eastes also prescribed and dispensed whatever medicine/pills were required as there was no pharmacy in the town.

The dentist was something else. Mr Brown, a Scotsman, had a surgery close to the railway arches in Chippenham. We used to catch the bus up to Chippenham with tension mounting as we approached our destination. Our treatment was all paid for by the NHS and in those days there were no injections for routine fillings. I can still remember today the rather laboured hum of a slow speed drill that gradually removed any rotten part of a tooth. For some reason there was always something to do upon inspection of our teeth, and it was the era of 'drill and fill' which lasts with me today. In my early years we used a toothbrush and Gibbs solid toothpaste in a small tin. You wetted the brush and then rubbed it on the solid dry powder to create an abrasive paste that was transferred to your mouth to clean your teeth. In later years pre-mixed toothpaste was available, which made the job easier and more pleasant.

Schools

I started school at the Infant School at the top of the town, in St Martin's Lane. The School was adjacent to the large Congregational Chapel which was on the corner of St Martin's Lane and the High Street. There was no nursery school to attend in those days, so we all arrived at the Infant School unaccustomed to sitting at a desk and listening carefully. Given that Anita and I had birthdays in September, it was always a question when to start or change schools, and whether we were ready or not to make the change. We went to Infant School when we were five years old as our sixth birthdays arose in the September. Mrs Wilson was our teacher and we spent two years at the School. Mrs Wilson was a dear lady, usually dressed in a matching skirt and coat, who as a reward for getting an answer correct or doing something when asked, gave out sweets, which was quite an incentive. If you fell, she applied some yellow ointment to the graze, presumably some sort of antiseptic, to make things better. She covered the basics of reading, writing and arithmetic, and generally induced in us a level of discipline. For Mum it was quite a lot of walking from one end of the town to the other, in all weathers.

Eventually it came our turn to attend Primary School, which was situated in the centre of the town adjacent to Weir Lane. It was a Church School so was run along

Christian lines of thinking and had three teachers and classes.

The class for the youngest pupils was run by Miss Tugwell, at the time a young teacher, who I was fortunate enough to meet again in May 2016 when there was a reunion for all those who had attended the School in the 1950s. Then in her 80s, she remembered me and was interested in what I had done in my life.

The middle class was run by Mrs Edwards who lived in the town, just down from the butcher's shop towards the School. She was middle aged and quite a disciplinarian, and was also known as 'Jammy Edwards' for what reason I do not know. Sometime after we had left the School she retired and I do not know what became of her.

The upper class was run by Mr Frank Davies, the Headmaster and he was also quite strict. In those days, a rap over the knuckles was still allowed, as well as bellowing out at unruly pupils. Occasionally a blackboard duster was thrown as a missile at pupils disturbing the class. We sat, I recall, at rather old-fashioned high desks with an integral seat, in ranks across the classroom. The desks had ink wells that were not used as all writing was done with a fountain pen, which was always messy to fill and avoid splodges on your pages, even if you had avoided bending the nib!

The School had a playground at the back and outside toilets that you were only encouraged to use during break times. During winter numerous plumbing problems arose and certainly nobody hung about given the al fresco offering!

So, what did we learn at School? There was great emphasis on reading, writing and arithmetic (the descriptor mathematics was only used in secondary school). Improving vocabulary was important. Nature studies (science) featured significantly and we studied trees and their leaves, various plants, tadpoles, frogs and toads, birds, lizards etc. all linked to the local environment in which we were growing up. Occasionally we went on nature walks to gather raw material for our work. History was taught, although very much from a British Empire (Commonwealth) perspective. I still recall today, Clive of India and General Wolfe who established a British hold on Canada and pushed the French back to Quebec. We covered the history of the UK from the Stone Age through to the Second World War, which was still a recent memory for all parents of children in the School. Geography and exploration were covered, again from an Empire building perspective, and the classical European explorers - Marco Polo, Magellan, Vasco de Gama, John Cabot all featured. Arts and Crafts, and painting were also covered, with mementos being proudly presented at home to Mum and Dad.

My years at School were marked by the traditional individual School photograph taken by the touring school's photographer. Mum saved these pictures religiously and I have a full set showing my progression through the School.

Time in the playground was spent in short trousers playing football, occasionally fighting and playing conkers. Mr Davies paid some of the more senior boys to dig his garden during holiday periods. The garden was adjacent to the playground and I think Mr Davies got the better part of the deal, as the garden was quite overgrown as I recall, and some heavy digging was required.

School trips were made to London to see the sights and understand our national heritage. These trips were of long duration and, before motorways, used to take five hours in both directions, with several stops to use the facilities or cope with the travel sickness of quite a few of the children. We were packed off by Mum with all our sandwiches, cakes and drinks to keep us fuelled for the day. I must say the trips gave me an early understanding of London and the layout of all that the city had to offer, which later, when I attended the International Science Fortnight, proved of enormous benefit. On these London trips we took in such sights as Buckingham Palace, Westminster Abbey, Houses of

Parliament, St Paul's Cathedral, Tower of London, Museums and Art Galleries.

Meals were brought into the School, but I do not recall having those meals, rather both Anita and I went back home for lunch. We played games to and from the classroom - including not standing on the cracks in the pavement for fear of being eaten by the crocodile or laying against the wall every time a lorry passed by to avoid being notionally crushed. Sherbet fountains or liquorice laces were occasionally purchased in Hayes shop, on the corner of the Market Place, on the way back home.

Time at Primary School was signalled as coming to an end with the Eleven Plus examination, which had to be taken before going on to a secondary school. Prior to the examination itself, each student took an Intelligence test and after Anita and I had taken this test, it was agreed that we would be held back a year as it was felt that we were too young to proceed. On the second time of asking we progressed to the full examination, which Anita passed to go to Kingswood Grammar School. I was on the cusp of pass/fail and was interviewed at Kingswood Grammar School with Mum in attendance. After the interview it was felt that I would thrive better at a new school that had just become available, Rodway Technical High School. More of this opportunity in a moment, but it was a saving grace that having not passed my Eleven Plus examination I did go to Rodway, although at the time it did not feel that way.

After leaving Primary School we were presented with a bible to commemorate the School being 100 years old. Looking back at my time at Primary School, I enjoyed my time there and the subjects that we covered. I probably did not realise how valuable my learning had been, but I had understood that a level of work was required to ensure a good outcome, i.e. I had learned how to learn and that has stayed with me.

****

Onwards to secondary school...

Rodway Technical High School was located on the common at Mangotsfield. I accessed the School via a bus to Warmley and then a link bus over to Mangotsfield. The School had been established as offering a range of more practical subjects compared to the Grammar School, but set itself academically above the other local secondary school at Oldland Common. The School was progressively filling up its year groups having opened four or five years in advance of my arrival. Mr Hughes was the Headteacher and the uniform was grey and wine red. Caps were worn and boys were in short trousers for the first three years, although I recall in the third year, and being over six feet in height, that long trousers were allowed.

Unfortunately, with playing football the knees of long trousers were frequently torn and patches were required to be applied by an inventive mother.

Corporal punishment was still administered at School by the Head, Mr Hughes, and his Deputy, Mr Stokes, when canning boys over the backside was still allowed. In classrooms a variety of largely non-contact techniques to enforce discipline were used, but I recall Mr Stokes pulling upward on boys' sideburns to painful effect. All would not be allowed in today's school environment.

The School was by today's standards quite small with 700-800 pupils, including a Sixth Form. Coming from Marshfield Primary School, which had about 90 pupils, the School seemed massive when I arrived, and there was no induction process or gradual start as there would have been today.

Early on I struck up a friendship with Paul Moores who came from Hanham. We have stayed in contact over the years and whilst at School we visited and stayed in each other's homes, as well as sharing a holiday with some other boys from the School, including Chris Boltz, Phil Loud and Alan Millett.

Sport at secondary school I cover elsewhere, and it was an important and large part of what secondary school was for me. It provided a bridge from earlier days in Marshfield and a standing in the School other than that arising through academic achievement. One aspect of sport not covered elsewhere was when there was a double PE period and the weather was so awful that we could not go outside, and the opportunity was taken by the School for instruction in ballroom dancing. Boys were lined up one side of the hall and girls on the opposite side and when the music started boys were instructed to take their partners. Nobody moved to take part in whichever dance was to be practiced, which led to an automatic pairing of boys and girls. At the time I think nobody really enjoyed these afternoons, but later in life there were many times that I was grateful for the instruction provided - Quick Step, Foxtrot and Gay Gordon's here I come!

Various dances and discos were held at the School. These all involved the 'modern' music of the day - Beatles, Rolling Stones Chubby Checker and Adam Faith.

The School offered opportunities to learn a musical instrument, play in the orchestra, sing in the choir and to perform in a play. I did not avail myself of any of these. My speech impediment did not encourage me to perform on the stage and I was not a natural musician or singer. Besides, there was so much else to do with sport and academic work to the fore. I did however attend several Shakespeare plays, which improved my understanding of the poet and might explain the subsequent performance in my English Literature examination.

Academically, when I first arrived at School, and for the three years before options needed to be chosen to progress to Ordinary 'O' levels, I found that I was able to perform best in Mathematics, Science, History, Woodwork/Metalwork and Geography. Subjects where I was not so good were English, French and Music. Encouragingly, I was awarded School prizes in each of these three years, which was a real motivator. The books I received at that time I still have today and chart important milestones in the much larger steps I would take in subsequent years. One book particularly remains vivid in my memory in describing the history of science through the ages, up to the mid-1900s, with all the famous scientists recorded. This book undoubtedly inspired me to look more carefully at science as a career.

School photographs at the time were taken of the whole School, with a clockwork camera, with the idea that each student could be seen. Some students were seen twice as they ran around the back of the assembled group and looking back at these photos it is great to still identify faces and wonder what happened to them all?

As now, Parent evenings were held with your teachers to inform parents of progress. I am not sure who was more nervous, Mum and Dad or me. With generally good reports and some areas for improvement, most evenings had a positive outcome. When it came to subject options to be chosen at the end of the third year, I think I largely chose them myself and pointed myself unashamedly towards a science and technology future. I chose to take a Maths 'O' level one year early in the fourth year, and to follow that with Additional Maths, English Language, English Literature, French, Physics, Chemistry and Technical Drawing examinations in the fifth year. To explain my choices, English Language and French were mandatory passes to be able to study a science at university. English Literature I was quite good at and Geography and History were not available options in the mix that I could choose, but later would always be subjects of interest throughout my life. Technical Drawing was a new subject to be studied and was seen as 'one up' from the subjects of Woodwork or Metalworking. We also had some rather advanced, for the time, adjustable sliding drawing boards in a dedicated Technical Drawing room. The subject was taught by the Head, Mr Hughes.

So, with options chosen there was the serious business of performing well in the selected subjects. At the end of the Fourth Form I took my first 'O' level and secured a Grade 1 pass. I was thrilled. Results were simply taped to the inside of the School glass doors for all to read, with no counselling available for distraught students or guidance on next steps. Eventually I received a letter in the post confirming the outcome.

The Fifth Form arrived with the pressure of exams arising at the end of the year and choices to be made about your future. Options were to leave school or to stay on in the Sixth Form? The latter was what I wanted to do, but for Mum and Dad there was the question of continuing to support me. I do not recall a specific conversation about finances, rather an osmosis of understanding that staying at School was the course for me to take and they were supportive. At the same time Anita left Kingswood Grammar School to embark on a career in the Civil Service/Inland Revenue.

Options chosen for the Sixth Form were to take Pure and Applied Maths 'A' level in the Lower Sixth and then Pure Maths, Chemistry and Physics in the Upper Sixth. As it turned out, I also took the Special 'S' Level exams at that time in Chemistry and Maths.

Recalling the 'O' level subjects, all was going well although French was a struggle. The subject teacher, Miss French no less, had a class full of budding scientists who knew they had to pass the exam, but were not necessarily naturals at the subject. We had a modern language laboratory for our use, which had been built to support the Anglo-French Concorde project for use outside of School hours by engineers and scientists, but it was a struggle. Anyhow results day confirmed that I had passed French and had obtained grade one in other subjects, except English Language in which I had failed having obtained a Grade 1 in English Literature! A retake therefore loomed in November, which I passed and I also took the 'Use of English' examination in the Upper Sixth and passed.

An important opportunity availed itself when I was invited to attend the International Youth Science Fortnight during the summer of 1967 in London. This was undoubtedly a seminal moment in defining that I wanted to progress to a science, engineering and technology career. I was the sole representative from Gloucestershire and for a fortnight we were immersed in many aspects of science, engineering and technology. We stayed in a University Hall of Residence at Russell Square, with lectures on the Embankment at the Royal College of Electrical Engineers, at Imperial College and at Kings College. We had an impressive visit to Hawker Sidley to see a Harrier Jump Jet, which had just been developed at that time, and they gave us our own ground and take-off display. Besides the mass of subjects covered, it was an opportunity to compare myself with others who were there from all over the world. There were some very bright people attending, but I felt I could hold my own in their company. I was immensely proud to have been selected to represent my School, my County and my Country.

In the Lower Sixth I was selected to be a prefect, which involved supporting staff in keeping discipline around the School. The Sixth Form prefects could issue their own detentions, which had to be supervised and could involve either time during the School day or after School depending upon the severity of the misdemeanour. Tasks given to students in detention were not very inventive and usually involved writing out fifty or a hundred times 'I must not….'. In the Upper Sixth I was selected as Head Boy, which was a big surprise to me, and with that came responsibility for organising and galvanising the prefects as required. Additionally, the Sixth Form had been given a separate room for our use at the southern end of the School site. Ensuring good operation of that area and the associated 'tuck' room - crisps and Coca Cola (healthy options only!) was part of the brief. I recall that Lynda Watkin was Head Girl, with Susan Cole her deputy and my own deputy was Peter Randall. It was my first significant leadership role and I think I acquitted myself reasonably well. There were no rebellions or coups and discipline was good, so I must have been doing something well.

Teachers in the Sixth Form to whom I must give many thanks to for helping me achieve the results that I did were Chemistry (Mr Pascoe and Mr Jones), Physics (Mr Dyer and Mr Williams), Pure Maths (Mr Williams) and Applied Maths (Mr Nicholson). At the end of the Lower Sixth I obtained a Grade 'A' for Pure and Applied Maths, followed at the end of the Upper Sixth with Grade 'A's' in Chemistry, Physics and Pure Maths as well as Passes at 'S' level for Chemistry and Maths.

During the Upper Sixth there was the important question of what next and if that meant going to university, which one and how to finance my time at university? Recalling that I was the first of my family to think about going to university it was new to Mum, Dad and I, but we worked our way through the bureaucracy. It was still the time when a grant could be made for a living allowance for students, depending upon parental income. Given Dad's income, some support was available and Mum and Dad agreed to top up to the required amount. Academic fees were covered directly by the Gloucestershire Education Services.

In terms of which university to apply to via the UCAS process, I did not apply to Oxbridge as I did not think I was good enough to be accepted - more of that in a later book perhaps. Having been in London at The International Youth Science Fortnight, I fancied applying to a London college and so I applied to Imperial and Kings Colleges, with Chelsea College as a back-up. I also applied to universities in Southampton, Birmingham and Leicester. I received offers from the London Colleges, but I thought they were quite demanding, considering that I had one 'A' level already at grade 'A'. In retrospect the grades requested of two grade B's was not too demanding. I kept Birmingham and Imperial College in London under consideration, then out of the blue Birmingham offered me an interview for a scholarship. I attended and after the interview was given an Open Entrance Scholarship. This was significant and represented income of about a quarter of my first year living grant. They also dropped my entrance exams to passes in Chemistry and Physics. They were keen to have me, and I was keen to go. Mr Pascoe was particularly pleased as he was an old alumnus of the University of Birmingham.

One innovation in the Sixth Form was that for one afternoon a week we could choose a subject not related to our likely career path. Several boys, including me, chose to do Cookery as we did not fancy living on beans on toast for our whole time at university. We had a very patient lady teaching us who normally took 'Domestic Science' classes. It was great fun and we learned to bake bread, cook a significant Sunday roast etc. which helped us prepare for the future, although beans on toast still featured.

Prizes continued throughout the Sixth Form and were a constant motivation. To say it clearly, my secondary education was transformative for me and helped me on my life's journey. I remain eternally grateful. Many students that I was at School with, attended further education after leaving the School and all had the opportunity to learn and make more of themselves. The mid-sixties were a time of Harold Wilson's 'White-Hot Technology' thrust and Britain was investing heavily in science, engineering and technology, so it was a good time to be heading in that career direction.

I recently went back to the School with Paul Moores to attend a reunion. As with all things, change has occurred and comparisons with the past cannot helpfully be drawn. The School is now teaching students up to sixteen years of age, with no sixth form and is much bigger (probably twice the number of pupils compared to when I attended). It is twinned with another local school that provides sixth form facilities. The grounds have been significantly built upon, although the running track remains. It was good being there with some alumni of the same vintage as myself and some even older. Amongst that group there was a lot of goodwill and I gained a sense of where the School is presently with a lot of the values from a previous era still in place. Thank you once again to Rodway Technical High School.

Sport

Sport was something that occupied a lot of my time and passion growing up in Marshfield. As a youngster, being tall was a major advantage in the main sports of football and cricket, and gave me the opportunity to step up into the more senior town teams at an earlier stage than would otherwise have been the case. From a young age there was a natural progression from small scale games to more organised team games and thence to regulated games. But I get ahead of myself.

From early in my life, playing with a ball, either kicking, throwing or batting, were things that Mum, Dad and all relatives encouraged in me, whether on the lawn at home or on playing fields. Dad had been a keen sportsman, playing for the town at cricket and football, but with the arrival of Anita and I his participation in sports ceased. I guess, however, he wanted to ensure that a love of sport was passed on to me.

The Rec, or Withymead Recreation Ground to give its full name, which had been acquired from Major Pope (owner of Ashwicke Hall just south of the town) was a significant asset. It is located on the south east side of the town at the back of the housing estate, and originally had tennis courts located up towards the 'Barn' end of the site, but these were subsequently built on. The Rec was the gateway to Cloud Wood,

Marshfield Wood, Doncombe Brook and the Ringswell water treatment plant which were south and further east than the Rec.

A vivid memory, when I must have been only five or six, was on Christmas Day going around to the Rec with Dad, with me dressed in my new Christmas present which was a full Bristol Rovers football kit. The shirt was several sizes too big - to allow for growth - and the boots were the old leather type that came up around your ankles and took some breaking in. However, I was not going to admit to that on such a special morning. (The boots after cleaning were made supple and waterproof with Dubbin wax, a thick Vaseline type material, and the studs on the bottom of the boots were made of laminated leather with three nails sticking out. These were hammered into the leather sole of the boot and occasionally they came through the sole which meant a bit of levelling off was needed to avoid painful damage to your feet). I also had a leather ball, which, as those of that vintage will recall, would soak up water and become progressively heavier with further use. When heading this type of ball, it was like heading a very heavy Christmas pudding and required a positive move of your head onto the ball. (Sad to say it can easily be understood that such balls could well have caused damage to the brain that only appears in later life). I thought I was the 'bee's knees' in my Bristol Rovers kit. For those who do not understand the decision as to whether you supported Bristol Rovers or City, this was really determined largely by where you lived. Those living north or east of Bristol tended to support the Rovers and those who lived west and south the City. Once teams were selected, it was a lifetime of despair or joy that you could look forward to. Later in life, when living in Malaysia, I recall patiently explaining to the locals why I supported Bristol Rovers (who?) and not one of the topflight Premier League teams. I think they thought I was mad!

Bristol Rovers were at the time in the Second Division of the English League - there being no Premier League. Rovers played at Eastville in the centre of a dog racing track, and close to the gas works - hence Rovers being today called the 'Gas Heads'. As a treat, I occasionally went to matches, usually with Uncle Percy and his son Michael. They had a car and we parked a fair distance from the ground and walked the rest of the way. Crowds in those days stood on the terraces and even for the Rovers, gates of 30,000 were quite common. Later I recall one game on 4th April 1961 when the Rovers beat Liverpool 4-3. It was magical. Two goals from Bobby Jones and one each from Hooper and Jarman secured the result. Both clubs have since then had vastly different paths. Rovers other nickname was the Pirates, reflecting the maritime history of Bristol. The club was founded in 1883, as the Black Arabs, changing their name to Bristol Rovers in 1899 and being admitted to the English league in 1920.

Organised sport was not undertaken at either Infant or Primary School, so that left all children to look towards the senior teams that played in the town, in the hope that one day they could join them and represent the town. However, watching matches was not the same as participating in them and so depending on the season, and who turned up, ad hoc games were organised on the Rec, with temporary goalposts or wickets established, and reputations made and lost. Team selection was always contentious with alliances being formed and broken. It made for a competitive environment and when returning home in your 'playing clothes', you and the clothes were somewhat dirtier from good use.

The Pink 'Un and its successor the Green 'Un newspapers arrived on a Saturday night, to give the football results that otherwise could be heard on the radio before television had been introduced. It was important for your 'street credibility' that you were up to date on the football news and could rattle off all sorts of statistics. In a way it also opened up the geography of the UK because understanding where teams played, for example Partick Thistle, was a must know in the banter about the game during the following week.

Collecting cards of famous sportsmen (not women at that time I am afraid) was de rigour. The cards came in tea, cigarette and cereal packages and were mounted in albums. I am sure the cards increased sales of the products concerned and I was forever chasing Mum and Dad to ensure I had the latest cards, even if that meant pre-opening packets! It also led to an active market in card swaps, with no money changing hands, but rare cards were swapped for several other cards. No doubt there were always a few cards that were as rare as 'hen's teeth' to keep you buying the product.

****

This utopian world of sport continued through to the time that I attended secondary school at Rodway Technical High School, where sport became more organised and varied. Within the School there was a house system within which sport was organised and I was in Berkeley House, with the other Houses being Manor, Blaise and Badminton. Below this level there were PE lessons, which were designed to ensure that all pupils had some exercise. If you were looking to represent the School, then there were additional practice sessions after lessons. These practice sessions presented a challenge as it meant missing the connecting bus over to Warmley to get home on time. I therefore either had to catch the train, which was still operating at that time, or undertake a 3-mile hike over to Warmley. Invariably it meant getting home past 6 pm.

At Rodway I participated in lots of sports, with special mention of football, cricket, hurdles, hammer throwing and cross country. My PE teachers during my time at the School were Mr House and Mr Arnold. Football was a natural extension of activities in Marshfield. I was selected for football duties from the first year, as was Paul Moores my school mate, and I played throughout my time at School except for the years when I was doing my Saturday morning butcher's round. I played right back and occasionally centre back, and we were a force to be reckoned with against the local schools that we played. Competitive instincts got out of hand in several matches. One notable match against Sir William Romney's School, Tetbury was abandoned when one of our players encouraged another of our players to 'get him' indicating one of the opposition players. The referee decided that this was not in the spirit of the game and so the match was abandoned. We had put six goals into their net by this stage! On another occasion the whole team was suspended for an incident at Merrywood Grammar School when we felt that they were giving our goalie Peter Milton a hard time. We chased their team around their school after the match attempting to exact justice, which we never managed to achieve. Anyhow at the whole school assembly on the Monday morning, the story of what had happened was retold and the team were duly suspended for several weeks for very ungentlemanly conduct. That said, Rodway teams were amongst the best of the local schools and games continued to be keenly contested.

Besides playing football for the School, I was fortunate enough to be selected to represent Gloucestershire, although I was never good enough to be selected for the first team and played in the second team.

Within School, as I explained earlier, there was a House structure and Paul and I were the mainstay of our group in the inter-house football team. We never quite won the Inter House Cup, with Manor House always having a slightly stronger team, but were strong contenders throughout.

Whilst playing football at School I was eventually selected during my teens to join the Marshfield senior team. This meant playing on a Saturday morning at School and then in the afternoon for Marshfield, so quick movement between locations was called for. Again, I usually played right back and we played in a Wiltshire League and then in the First Division of a Bath League. Travelling around local villages generated a good perspective of the local area and local rivalries, particularly so when playing Colerne village team, who invariably had a couple of 'ringers' playing from the RAF camp that was still active at the time. These chaps were super fit and gave us a bit of a run around. However, our secret weapon was to start braying like a donkey if times got tough and we were a few goals down, causing the Colerne team to lose their cool and invariably the game would swing our way. The reference to donkeys was the tale that a donkey had been buried upside down in the centre of the village and hence the football team were known locally as 'Colerne Kick Donkeys'. Andrews coaches took the Marshfield football teams, in which I played, to away games with players and supporters all aboard.

Part way through my teens, a Marshfield youth football team was started by Paddy Henderson, who was married to Mauve Field. She had grown up next door to us and her parents still lived at no. 2 Council Houses. Matches were played on Sundays and Paddy, as his name suggests, was an Irishman who had connections with RAF Colerne. He worked extremely hard to make a success of the youth football and that provided more experienced players coming into the senior town team. Paddy was a little eccentric and quick to fall out with people, so he never received the recognition he deserved for starting and sustaining a worthy town activity.

****

Football is a winter game and during the Summer, cricket was the game to be playing. Again, as soon as I attended Rodway School, I was selected to join the School cricket team and stayed through the years, apart from my years of being a butcher's boy in Marshfield. However, cricket flourished in the town and at the age of thirteen or so I found myself on either a Saturday or Sunday, or both, playing cricket having performed a couple of seasons as a scorer for the team. When I joined the team there were men still playing who had played with Dad, such as Ray Ball, Stan Greenhill, Jack Walter and Steve Aubrey and John Kitley, who were youngsters as Dad finished playing. My Uncle George was also playing and Aunty Evelyn used to sit in their car and watch the match. There was never a close relationship between us and it neither hindered nor helped my progress. Playing at home meant playing at the Rec and using the old pavilion was an education in etiquette - where to get changed and to make sure not to take sandwiches and cake before the opposition. In the early days I was invariably batting no. 9, 10, or 11, so it was a question of knocking off a few runs as best you could or defending 'to the death' as the reputation of the team was at stake to avoid losing the match. I did not bowl and in the field, like a lot of the other youngsters playing, I was deployed where there was plenty of leather to chase and save those precious runs. Occasionally a skyed ball would come your way and then it was a question of catching the ball - dark exchanges followed from the rest of the team if you dropped it. One 'catch' or rather 'non catch' sticks in my mind - at Blaise Castle, when Mum had come to watch, I was fielding at point and was in position to catch a ball lashed to the offside. Unfortunately, my hands did not close quickly enough and the ball hit me between my eyes. I was somewhat shaken up, but in those times there was not so much concern about concussion, so after a few overs I returned to carry on fielding. Mum never came to a match again.

At home matches we never entertained visiting teams at the local pub, but for away matches, and before drink drive laws were in place, there was always a drink or two to be taken, either at the home team's local or stopping on the way back. Team transport was provided by individuals with their cars and team members were generous in buying lads like myself a pint or two, so win or lose there was always a story to tell. As with football, the opportunity to get out and about in the locality was great. All games were arranged on a friendly basis and home and away games were reciprocated. Special mention should go to Doug Moules, who was our groundsman and umpire. Doug had an accident that left his hands damaged, however he could still push the mower across the square, mark out the white lines and officiate at the games. The outfield was cut by Les Chivers using tractor and gang mowers. Umpiring was an art form in our games, with some interesting decisions being made. Wicket keepers fielding close to the stumps encouraged the bails to unexpectedly fly off, with a nudge on a wicket, leaving the unsuspecting umpire with no other decision than to give the batsman out.

Marshfield Cricket Club frequently used the abbreviation MCC to suggest connections with the great and the good of the game. During the winter months, the club would attend the Peter Wight School of Cricket in Bath, on part of the site where Bath Cricket played. Transport was provided, so it was an opportunity mid-week to get some exercise and improve skills. Peter Wight, Somerset's most prolific post-war run scorer, set up the School and coached local cricketers after his playing days were over. The School has recently been knocked down to make way for student accommodation.

****

Rodway School introduced me to other sports, such as gym work, weights, cross country and athletics. Regarding cross country, the normal run was across Rodway Common, round past the Horseshoe pub, back past Carson Chocolate factory and up the hill past the railway station back to School. I did compete on one occasion in the South Gloucestershire cross country games, but rarely came in higher than eighth or ninth on a School cross country run. The only notable event on one occasion was returning exhausted, I reached for the nearest telegraph pole to support myself. As my hands slid down the pole, I sliced the bottom part of my hand open because some idiot had placed a razor blade in the cracks of the pole. I then had to take a trip to hospital to have eight or so stitches inserted. Fortunately, it was my left hand, and my studies were not much affected as handwriting was the order of the day then.

The School was fortunate in having a cinder running track and associated run ups to the various sand pits used for field events. The cinder provided a flat surface that allowed activities to continue during light showers, and in its time was state of the art, and serviced regional and national athletes from all over the West of England. We were fortunate to be able to run, jump and throw on such a good surface. With my long legs I was a natural for the high hurdles and that was my preferred race initially. I represented South Gloucestershire in several meetings at the hurdles, but never broke through beyond that level. As time went on and I continued to grow and fill out Mr Arnold, the PE Master, felt that Hammer Throwing would be a natural event for me. We had a 'cage' and throwing area within the track and so with my protective glove on my left hand I diligently practiced. There was of course some lack of congruence between running the hurdles and throwing the hammer, in that different physiques are required, so

I settled on hammer throwing in the end. I achieved the heady height of representing Gloucestershire at the West of England games in Exeter, but that was as far as I reached. There was talk about going further, but the effort and time involved were not compatible with my academic studies.

Hobbies and Pastimes

Like a lot of other boys, I followed an array of hobbies and pastimes that came and went over the years in Marshfield.

I joined Cubs in my pre-teenage years, with meetings held in the Church Hall, and wore a green jumper upon which all sorts of badges and regalia were accumulated. We had the obligatory scarf (grey and red as I recall) with the woggle to hold the scarf in position around the neck. Cubs did not involve camping away from home and quite a lot of the activity was based in the Church Hall itself. I progressed through a whole range of badges and became a 'sixer', leading a small group of more junior boys. I recall participating in the Flower Show parade with the Cubs and in 'bob a job week', when funds were raised. Some sponsors I recall were more reasonable than others when it came to what they expected for the 'bob'- one shilling or five pence in new money

Unfortunately, the town did not have a Scout troupe, the nearest one being in Wick, so I never honed my skills further, but then in a way the whole town was an 'outward bound' activity.

****

Today collecting birds' eggs (nesting) would be unacceptable, and in many cases illegal, but it was a normal activity for town lads in the fifties and early sixties to assemble a collection of bird's eggs. The education process started with the collection of cards from tea packets, PG Tips in our case, cereal packets, cigarette packets, comics or the like.

With nature all around, this inevitably graduated to exploring the environment to observe and listen to the birds on the cards and obtain the required egg to add to the collection. Information was carefully guarded about the rarer birds in the locality and trips with 'mates' sworn to silence on penalty of horrendous outcomes. Great treks to faraway barns, distant streams - they seemed like rivers at the time - and quite scary woods, at least when the sun was setting, greatly expanded my knowledge of the area. All of this was taking place within a four mile radius of the town, with longer outings involving a bike ride, hiding the bike and then scrambling to the required destination. Once there, other skills of climbing, clambering inside barns and manoeuvring under bridges were used to reach the desired nest.

Eggs were indeed taken from the nest, but there was some honour amongst the egg collectors. No more than one egg could be taken per nest and there always had to be one egg left in the nest.

Collections were then assembled in shoe boxes, or the like, with eggs placed on sand after the contents of the egg had been carefully emptied with a pin prick at either end and the contents blown out. On wet days these could then be shown to your mates and swaps arranged to complete collections.

By my middle teens I had grown out of egg collecting and passed my collection onto others.

****

Stamp collecting was a hobby I persisted with through my years in Marshfield, first collecting the stamps that arrived in the house and then broadening out to buy packets of stamps from all over the world, which was a great geography lesson. I very occasionally looked at stamps in the window of the Stamp and Coin shop that today is still on Pulteney Bridge in Bath, but only rarely purchased. I did receive as presents, Stanley Gibbons envelopes of stamps, that contained stamps from all over the world, which further expanded my collection and knowledge of countries.

Coins were also collected, although funds were limited, and I started with the lower denomination ones of a farthing, halfpenny, and penny (all old currency). They became the basis of my coin collection today and were added to with a few silver coins, given to me by Grampy Lewis and Mum and Dad's collection.

Comics, magazines and newspapers were read. The Dandy, Beezer, Hotspur and others were my favourites, and as I grew up I took an interest in newspapers.

We always had radio in the house with television coming along before our teen years.

Card and board games were widely played and have provided a love of competitive interaction throughout my life, as well as teaching me to count, weigh up risk, spell (not so well) and learn about money.

Conkers was a seasonal pastime governed by the availability of the fruit from the horse chestnut tree. The game itself involved testing your conker against opponents who were determined to destroy your conker. Individual conkers were skewered through with a hole and a length of string with a knot at the end, to secure the conker. Then taking turns, each player was allowed one strike of their conker on the opponent's conker. This process continued until one conker fell off the string and the opponent was declared the winner. Conkers were progressively called one'ers, two'ers etc. depending upon the number of conkers that they had managed to destroy. I cannot recall more than six'ers. Great lengths were undertaken to achieve an all-conquering conker, including baking and soaking in vinegar and subsequently drying off. The technique to attack your opponent's conker was also important, as well as your aim. A short swift stroke was called for, hitting the 'meat' of your opponent's conker to achieve maximum effect. I do not recall being an expert at the game and did not have a conker that was more than a two-er or three-er.

Youth Club was something that I was involved in from my mid-teens onward. In the town the club was run initially in the Church Hall and then in what was the Royal British Legion building further up in the High Street. (This building had previously been the Unitarian Chapel). Anita, my sister went to the club with her friends well before me and introduced me when I eventually arrived. It was run, I recall, by Mrs Lake whose daughter was a similar age to Anita. There was music available with the occasional disco and even less frequently a band attending. Table tennis was also available and you could buy Coca Cola and crisps. Not much dancing went on, but we all thought that we had a 'night out' and parents were no doubt pleased to see us home.

Notable events at local villages were the Badminton Horse Trials, the car racing at Castle Combe and the RAF Tattoo at Colerne. The latter was held on an annual basis until my teenage years and involved a tremendous display of parked aeroplanes from the second world, as well as the occasional missile. The Cold War was still underway and there were air displays of all types of aircraft. As a youngster it certainly garnered an interest in technological exploits, if not militaria. As for other venues, it was a question of biking across to the site, parking up and then using local knowledge to sneak in. When the Tattoos ended I did not return to Colerne until my later teens, when big band dances were held with not much dancing but plenty of drinking.

The car racing at Castle Combe I only attended once or twice. Besides car racing, there was motorcycle racing, but as with now, the interest in watching vehicles zoom around a circuit without knowing all the details behind them, was not that enthralling for me. There were few crashes either, so no headlines to report.

Badminton Horse Trials were somewhat different and on a completely different scale to that found today. There was plenty going on around the circuit with loudspeakers announcing who was jumping. The number of shopping stalls was much fewer compared to what is seen today, but intriguing enough for a town lad to spend some time viewing them all.

Motorcycle 'scrambling' was something that I was introduced to by Cousin Bryan. It was in my mid-to-late teens that scrambling - a cross country motorcycle race over a closed course of rough terrain with steep hills and sharp curves - became popular and Bryan used to take me to 'meets' on the back of his motorcycle. It was an introduction to another world and depending upon the weather could be quite dangerous. It always involved a lot of noise from the two stroke engines in the motorcycles as they fought for traction, with a lot of dirt and mud being thrown around. As far as I was aware nobody was killed during these events as I guess speeds were limited by the terrain, but injuries to the riders were not uncommon. For me it was exciting riding with Bryan, as a pillion passenger, on his motorcycle and being at the events themselves.

Marshfield winters are often talked about as being severe and certainly I recall most winters with some snow. The snow, depending upon its severity, could mean that you could not get to School and winter sports were possible including snowballing, building a snowman and sledging. Sledging took place at Blue Park, which was accessed via a pathway in Little End, just down from the Vicarage. Dad made several sledges for us and there was a lot that went into the design, including depth of runners, metal strips on runners, size of sledge etc. The sledges were always sturdy, and rather heavy, if not always quite as aerodynamic or should I say 'snow-dynamic' as would have been beneficial. Numerous snowball fights were the norm and great fun was had as well as lots of calories burnt off.

****

Fishing was not a major activity during my youth. Whilst Marshfield has lots of rain, there are very few 'rivers' within striking distance of the town, which is probably a consequence of being on top of the hill. There are streams, particularly those at Shire Hill or through Cloud Wood and Marshfield Wood, but these do not support sizable fish or fish populations. Fishing was therefore confined to what could be caught in a net and placed in a jar. I would also include the occasional amphibian - frogs, toads and newts. Tadpoles and sticklebacks were common, but keeping them alive was always a challenge as chlorine levels in the water from the tap seemed to finish them off quickly.

****

Marshfield being a rural community, was surrounded by fields, copses and woods and these became a natural playground for all the boys of the town. In those care-free days we would go off for hours at a time, rarely informing Mum or Dad where we were going. On some occasions a bike ride was undertaken before hiking onward. I guess in retrospect we operated within a four mile radius of the town most of the time, but some of the journeys felt like real exploration. On the west side of the town we visited Bulls Hills and despite its name there never seemed to be bulls around. There were a few barns and if you walked far enough you almost reached Lansdown. To the north of the town having passed 'The Castle' farm and veering east, you came to Shire Hill and the stream at the bottom. To the east was

Cloud Wood and Marshfield Wood and to the south was the farmland that eventually reached to Ashwicke Hall. Before the farmland there was Ringswell, which housed the local water treatment works. This was our playground. Cloud Wood and Marshfield Wood were places where dens could be built and returned to time and time again. There was great pride in acting out the 'woodsman' skills that we saw on cowboy films, the adventures of Davy Crockett and those which we read about in comics. The woods could be a scary place as the sun was setting and the shadows lengthening. The gravel road back to the town was long and wound around, and you were never quite sure what was ahead of you and what was behind you. The solution was to run like the clappers until you reached the Rec playing fields!

What follows might seem a little weird and might explain a lot, but I used to, on my own, find great solace in lying flat in the fields, particularly when the grass was long, to gaze up on a summer's day and just watch the clouds go by. The shapes and images that could be imagined were limitless. There were armies marching across the sky, aeroplanes, giant animals, huge birds, people floating by, cars and many more objects. By half closing my eyes and fully relaxing I could float up into the sky and join some of the menagerie. I told you it was going to be weird and I can assure you no stimulants were involved, just an overactive young mind perhaps!

Around the town wildflowers blossomed as the seasons came and went, and knowing where these were to pick them for Mum was a treat. In the spring there were snowdrops, followed by primroses and a few crocuses. These were followed by bluebells, cowslips and buttercups as Spring turned to Summer.

Fruits could be found either growing wild or in gardens. The latter involved 'scrumping' and required being fleet of foot, having an extensive reach and hopefully not being caught. Eventually you could only eat so many apples, pears, plums, gooseberries (goosegogs) and blackcurrants in secret.

Wild fruit involved collecting rather small strawberries, crab apples which could be very bitter, sloes and damsons (for gin), blackberries and elderflower to make wine.

Collecting hazel nuts, especially from Cloud Wood and Marshfield Wood, was also a key Autumn activity. Nuts were kept until Christmas and then if you could use the nutcrackers and keep the nut locked in position, you might enjoy a tasty kernel dipped into salt. Mushrooms were always difficult, especially when one got to know that they could kill you, so I stayed away from collecting wild mushrooms, although these were widely collected by others.

Climbing trees was a pre-requisite for being able to join in some communal activity. One graduated over the years from small to larger and more complex trees, eventually mastering trees thirty foot high. I cannot recall one single child falling from a height and being harmed during my childhood. Climbing trees was essential for bird egg collecting, escaping from gangs on occasions and some games that involved covering a distance without touching the ground.

****

In my youth I felt that I belonged to a range of groups or gangs. I think for boys rather than girls, belonging to a group is more important than having a lot of friends. I had several friends into whose houses I would go on wet afternoons. I do not know why, but I seemed to go mainly to their houses rather than friends coming to our house. Gangs were replicated in school forms, year groups and houses, as well as sports teams. I was also content in my own company and being quite studious was happy opting out of some of the activity and re-joining when I wanted to. Up to my teen years I therefore probably had half dozen friends with tens of acquaintances.

Fighting in my early years was not uncommon and being on the large size I guess I did not come off too badly. However, there were some real scrappers in the town who seemed to exist to have a good fight and they had to be given as wide a berth as possible. Fighting lapsed by the mid-teens as I matured and there were better things to do.

****

Buzz arrows are, as I later found out, also known as Swiss, Dutch, Scotch or Gypsy arrows. Great energy went into the construction and throwing of buzz arrows to perfect the design. For those not in the know, a buzz arrow is named after the noise it makes in flight. It was constructed from a single piece of wood which could be a piece of timber, a cane, a very straight whip of hazel etc. with length varying from one foot up to about two feet. At one end the flights, usually made of cardboard but occasionally of feathers or plastic, were added on a cross-cut. At the other end the arrow was sharpened to a point, with occasionally a short nail added to 'balance' the arrow in flight. Just beneath the flights, a notch was made and a string with a single knot was wrapped around the shaft of the arrow at the notch. After notching, the remaining length of string was laid along the length of the arrow and pulled taught whilst holding the bottom of the arrow. To launch the arrow, the string was held in position and the arrow held between the thumb and the first two fingers. Then running in the direction you wanted the arrow to go, you performed an overarm whipping throw, pointing 45 degrees upward and released the bottom of the arrow using the string to hurl the arrow on its trajectory. Once the technique was perfected, considerable distances (the main criteria for success) could be achieved with 50-80 meters not being uncommon. The whole activity was fraught with danger as the arrows were not that controllable, but nobody that I knew was 'speared' by an arrow, although the occasional close thud as an arrow landed nearby was not unusual.

****

Summer holidays, particularly when at Primary School, seemed to be those long hot summers that we all remember through rose tinted glasses. Summer holidays were rather like long weekends, but an innovation for a few summers was a day camp run by the Hebron Hall at the Rec, which involved going back afterwards to the Hall. At the Rec competitive games such as egg and spoon, three-legged and sack, etc., races were organised to be followed by more theologically based events at the Hall. There was always a warning from home about being drawn away from the Church of England. One event in the Hall sticks in my mind when the dozen or so of us youngsters were offered one 'goody' to take from a basket which was passed around. The basket duly made its' way around and eventually came back to the minister with just the old potato left. The minister duly opened the potato to reveal a pound note, which then lead into a talk about 'all that glitters is not gold' and 'look beyond the obvious to reveal the inner rewards'. The lesson has stayed in my memory and if you find yourself in that situation, go for the old potato!

Epilogue

I have written this book during the COVID-19 outbreak in the UK in 2020 and had the time and space to reflect on my own childhood in Marshfield.

With time available I intend to continue to write the story of my life and cover the time I spent at university.

There is a quote from John Mark Green as;

'Everyone has a history.

What you do with it is up to you.

Some repeat it.

Some learn from it.

The really special ones use it to help others'

I hope that in some small way this book opens a window for you to reflect on your life and that you can think about your history and decide what that may mean for you.

The generosity and support of family, friends, teachers, and everybody I have met during my childhood in and around Marshfield is gratefully acknowledged with many thanks.

Acknowledgements

I would like to thank all of those who have contributed to this book and particularly my wife Judith, my sister Anita Griffiths, my daughters Rebecca, Victoria and Harriet and my school friend Paul Moores - all of whom kindly agreed to review various drafts of the book and advise me of corrections and edits. That being the case all errors and omissions in the book are to my account only. I would be grateful to hear of any and apologise in advance if any offence has been caused.

I would also like to thank Carolyn A Williams author of 'Toll to Toll and Beyond'- a History of Marshfield in Words and Pictures. Her book is a source of fascinating history and stories about Marshfield and I have quoted several sections about the history of the town in my text for which I am grateful for her permission to use.

Thank you also to Ian S Bishop author of 'Around Marshfield-Then and Now', and 'Return to Marshfield'. I am grateful for his permission to quote from 'Introduction to Around Marshfield-Then and Now', regarding the history of the town.

If I have not mentioned you specifically by name, please accept my general thanks to all I have known and loved in my lifetime.